AF575752

The Intimate Beauty of a
Japanese Courtyard

The Intimate Beauty of a Japanese Courtyard

Contents

Introduction

The harmony of garden and house

Since ancient times, Japanese people have lived in harmony with nature through the four seasons. At times, the elements became menacing forces against which they fought, but their strong cultural upbringing conditioned them to always love and respect nature, and adapt to it, and so they did. This love for nature, and an almost sacred appreciation of its beauty, is seen throughout Japan's history in the many traditional gardens that were constructed, some which are over thousands of years old today and still stand to captivate visitors with their exquisite "magic." They are not only remarkable in their landscapes and compositions, but also in their beauty, for many transform through the passing days to share the changing seasons with visitors, often in blooms of pink in spring and crowns of auburn blush in autumn, painting magical sceneries that linger in memories.

The traditional garden is considered a Japanese artform and gardeners have always lavished great efforts toward reflecting nature and real landmarks in the intricate universe of the Japanese *niwa* (garden). They represent revered mountains with small hills and lakes with modest ponds; they plant trees of all sizes and thread pathways between them with stepping-stones, offering a place for visitors to pause and soak in the pleasing beauty of the garden.

The traditional Japanese garden has several key elements. *Chisen* refers to a stream, waterfall, or pond, often placed at the core of the garden. This arrangement also has a practical origin: in earlier times, water was usually drawn from rivers to create a pond or stream on the south side of buildings in order to ease the heat and humidity of the Japanese summer.

The ponds and streams in the *chisen* often originated from small waterfalls known as *niwataki*, which were typically 7 to 10 feet (2 to 3 meters) in height, with the arrangement of rocks determining the flow, speed, and beauty of the cascade, as well as its sound and volume. While European fountains often gush upward, the *niwataki* flows downward, creating significant differences in the appearance, reflections, sounds, and movement of the water.

Contrasting the traditional garden arranged with water features is the *karesansui*, or dry garden/landscape, which creates flowing water and ponds without their actual presence, instead using gravel and rocks to symbolize them. Raked gravel takes the place of water in a pond and is set by using a broom to create grooves that represent ripples and waves. Dry landscapes are arranged around the Zen concept *wabi sabi*, which is to take pleasure in the understated elegance of imperfection. Meandering around the sentiment of transience, *wabi sabi* acknowledges that nothing is permanent, and in a *karesansui*, persuades simple, tranquil arrangements that urge contemplation; the goal is to guide the observer toward realizing fulfillment beyond a material path, and on a more intimate level, self-acceptance. By connecting to the real world that is without pretense, one learns to be accepting of "what is," without dwelling on "what should be."

The *sekitei*, a fully rock garden, is similarly simplistic in appearance, but its arrangement is thoughtful and meticulous. Strict rules are adhered to with regard to the placement of each rock, as it is believed that gods dwell in rocks, too. They are used in odd numbers and placed in a triangular formation that has unequal sides, so as to create various depths in perception, thereby forming interactive compositions. Rocks are selected in varying shapes and sizes and different types of rocks are used for different purposes, such as paving, stepping-stones, and steps; the preference is usually natural, unprocessed rocks. The selected rocks are arranged and utilized as inspired by their shape and color, embracing, and even highlighting, their imperfections.

One distinctive use of rocks is to form stepping-stones or *tobiishi*. They are said to have been introduced by the sixteenth-century tea master, Sen no Rikyu in the teahouses he built.

Stepping-stones may be set in a variety of formations, each of which determines the path trailed through a garden, one's gait (how one moves through the garden), the number of steps one takes, and the views one sees—in essence, how one experiences the garden.

Through natural elements and age-old practices, Japanese gardens are designed to represent the phenomena and scenes of the native landscape. The art of landscape gardening is steeped in tradition and culture, like the Japanese tea ceremony, and, just like it, has had years to mature and refine itself, shaped by the rules within its fundamentals. Its evolution is also aligned largely with the country's historical periods. For example, the elaborate, extravagant gardens built for recreation and entertainment by aristocrats in the sixth century and Heian period ceded to more minimalist Zen gardens influenced by newly embraced Zen Buddhism. Smaller and simpler Zen gardens composed traditional garden elements such as ponds, bridges, islands, and waterfalls in rocks and gravel, and were built attached to temples to focus monks' meditation rituals. The later descent of the Azuchi-Momoyama period witnessed the thrive of tea gardens (*chaniwa*) that evoked the spirit of *wabi* (imperfect simplicity); these gardens usually featured stone lanterns and wash basins used for ritual cleansing prior to tea ceremonies. Stately gardens made their comeback in the Edo period, with garden designs departing from minimalist arrangements to combine elements of the tea garden with previous elaborations of ponds, islands, and hills around circular trails that afforded a variety of viewpoints to enjoy the garden.

The *tsuboniwa*, or courtyard garden, came to be as a pocket garden devised to bring nature into a space or home though it was small, and was usually enclosed, or under the overhang of roofs, within connected or adjacent buildings. When designing a house, no matter how small, *creating* a seamless connection with nature and the outdoor was essential and extremely important, and architects dedicated great effort toward linking the house (the indoor) with the courtyard (the outdoor). In Japanese, the phrase "*teioku ichinyo*," which literally means "garden and house, inseparable," expresses the perfect unification of inside and outside. The modest size of the *tsuboniwa* steers its design toward a simple, but meticulously considered execution that combines traditional garden elements from various garden iterations; this has become the foundation of the courtyard garden. However, by design, the *tsuboniwa* is not a garden to be entered, but a garden to be viewed—to sit, watch, and let thoughts drift with no concern of time.

Today, the *tsuboniwa* finds its place in many urban Japanese homes as intimate spaces of calm that place residents in the soothing embrace of nature. It exists in many variations, sometimes extending to imaginative green spaces that counter the formal definition of a courtyard garden, as the pages that follow will elaborate. No matter their design, placement or appearance, these courtyards (sometimes appearing more like gardens) still perform as intended—being points of calm and stillness amid the bustle, as they bring strokes of greenery into the modern home, to make the joy of nature's company a part of daily urban living.

To achieve the unification of garden and home, eaves come into play as a crucial element. Many variations of this architectural form exist, from the magnificent eaves of temples and shrines to the simple overhangs on small houses, with the essential function of protecting the walls from rain and wind. The beauty of their detailing and form is a noteworthy aspect of Japanese architecture. The depth of the eaves, the distance between their outer edge and the ground, and their design, all affect how one sees the garden. Eaves bear the brunt of the elements, so making structures strong enough to withstand the typhoons of summer, the snowstorms of winter, and various other climatic challenges that occur throughout the year is an intensely careful consideration. Beyond function, eaves also present a stage for the architect's creativity and skill to shine, as the projects 6 Roofs House, House OM, and T^3 will reveal.

Another construct that links the outdoor and the home is the *engawa*, which is a veranda under the eaves that faces the garden. It is here, in this intermediary sphere, that residents sit to experience the quiet rapture of the garden—feeling the wind brush their skin, listening to the birds singing, or simply gazing at the veil of rain trailing from the eaves. Although they remain within the home, they are able to enjoy the beauty of nature without restrictions. In the olden days, residents would compose poems about nature from the shelter of the *engawa*, however today, in a modern home, the *engawa* can be used in a variety of ways. Nagoya Courthouse, House YO, House Near Shigarakigu, and Loop Terrace highlight today's modern styles of the *engawa* and the different opportunities for respite and family time that they present.

The positioning of windows is another distinctive aspect as it allows the enjoyment of the courtyard. Many methods have been perfected to frame the outside world gracefully and beautifully—round windows to floor-level windows, to *yukimi shoji*, which are paper screens that can be pushed up at the lower half to reveal a glass pane. One walks through the house or sits on the tatami mat to enjoy the view through these windows, which may also frame "borrowed scenery," referred to as *shakkei*, such as a backdrop supplied by surrounding natural landscape. These views become "paintings" that change with the shifting sunlight and the soft glow of the moonlight at night. M4 features one such home that fills its interior with beautiful views of nature at every angle.

Japanese architecture is striking in that it is uncomplicated, yet captivating, often using the play of elements to ensure dimension within a space. One such approach is creating enchantment with shadows. Both the strong contrast of light and shadow, and the gradation of light—as one moves from a sun-drenched courtyard or garden to the softer light under the eaves, and finally into the darker recess of the house—contribute to this beauty. Junichiro Tanizaki writes about the appreciation for this particular kind of light in his essay, *In Praise of Shadows*, keenly aware of the beauty found in shadows that exist as the opposite of light. In my own architectural designs, I too am constantly conscious of bringing natural light indoors and balancing light with shadow. Tanizaki's book made me aware of just how attached I am to the idea of drawing out the beauty of shadows; I believe this approach to light is woven into the genetic core of Japanese people.

The shadows that form when the clean sunlight is segmented by windows, doors, walls, and columns bring a grace, moderation, and dignity to a space, settling it deeply in memory. The beauty and balance of shadow resulting from the unification of house and garden enhances a space and makes it soothingly pleasing. In the tiny universe that is a *tsuboniwa*, the natural world is reproduced in miniature, painstakingly and lovingly building an intimate connection between the outdoor and indoor. As both dimensions blend as one, the Japanese spirit, and home, is brought to life, celebrating and embracing nature, as has always been the way of Japanese people.

CUBO design Architect

H. Sunte

Location /
Shiga, Japan

Area /
2,831 square feet (263 square meters)

Completion /
2019

Design /
Hearth Architects

Photography /
Yuta Yamada

Minakuchi House

Perpetual portraits of nature

Set along an old streetscape in Minakuchi-juku, the fiftieth of the fifty-three stations (olden rest areas) along the coastal Tokaido route (one of the five routes of the Edo period connecting Kyoto to Edo), this house is among the smaller homes in the Shiga Prefecture. The narrow frontage and road beyond places the home's courtyard inside the house, in the southeast. This successfully overcomes ground issues of the site, while also ensuring the well-being of residents in relation to geomantic placement.

The outer wall is made of *Yakisugi* (burnt cypress cladding), which is a traditional Japanese material. The wood is charred on the surface so that the carbonization renders it waterproof and durable; this also protects it against insects and makes it fire-retardant.

The garden is a scene out of a painting, showcasing trees from Gifu. The main act is an Aodamo (Japanese ash) that is accompanied by other deciduous trees that display autumn foliage. An undergrowth of moss and ferns hedge a *funaishi*, also known as a ship stone (a slab of stone shaped like a ship), which traditionally carries symbolisms that include fortune, virtues, and even life experience.

The living and dining areas on the first floor face the courtyard and allow glimpses of nature through the day as residents go about their tasks, as do the children's room and the balcony beside the main bedroom on the second floor. A connection to the outdoor is never beyond reach, fostering an appreciation for nature and an unanimity with it. The feature tree is given wide visibility and can be seen from almost anywhere in the home; in the summer, its leafy foliage provides shade while allowing light to filter through, and in the winter, its sparse canopy puts up little resistance to the bleak winter light, so that sunshine still finds its way to the courtyard. As the trees quietly switch between green verdure and autumn blush, the seasons are experienced and enjoyed.

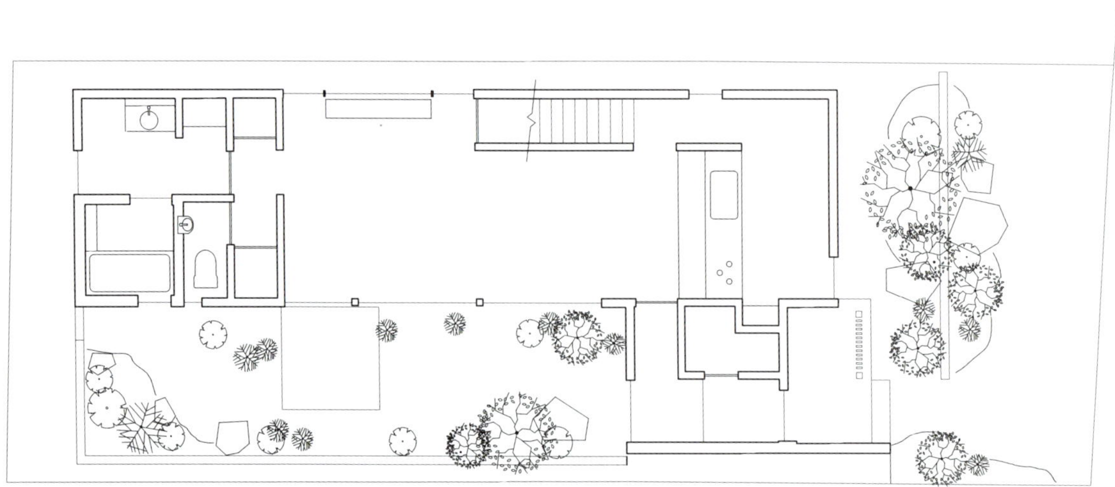

FIRST-FLOOR PLAN

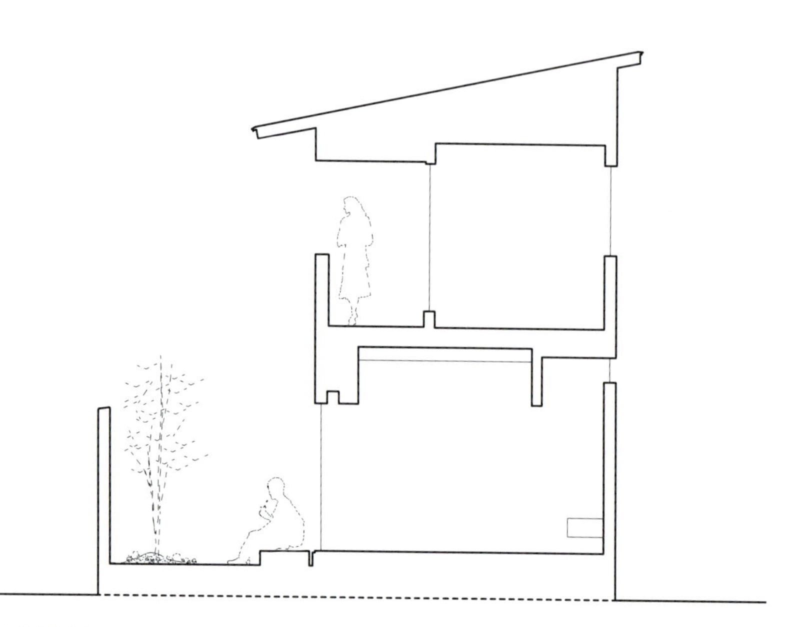

ELEVATION

Location /
Nagoya city, Aichi, Japan

Area /
5,070 square feet (471 square meters)

Completion /
2014

Design /
Takeshi Hosaka Architects

Photography /
Koji Fuji (Nacasa & Partners Inc.)

Nagoya Courthouse

Living scenes and scenery

Located approximately 0.6 miles (1 kilometer) west of Nagoya Castle, the site sits in a neighborhood that contains a mix of two-story houses and high-rise apartments. Summer in Nagoya brings about scorching temperatures with downpours that have been known to raise the water level to alarming heights.

Considering the climate, the home's location, and its high-rise neighbors, the design of the house locates the courtyard garden in the center. The courtyard is visible through glazed doors that sit under a non-linear roof line, which traces squarish protrusions and hollows, resembling an oriental square design. The roof line mimics the jagged skyline imposed with an erratic mix of high and low structures, and lends vision as an architectural style that cleverly creates shade against the blazing summer. The indoor and outdoor exist along a dismantled border, blending harmoniously to create a boundary that trails under roofed and unroofed portions. This half-inside–half-outside design makes room for a variety of living scenes: picking vegetables from the plot, children playing on the lawn, or relaxing in the shade to watch the sky welcome the evening.

The floor is 29.5 inches (75 centimeters) higher than the front street to protect against rising water during a heavy downpour. Diatom earth walls in the interior strengthen the home's connection to nature and the outdoors. A mortar footpath extends across the courtyard garden and connects different areas of the home through alternative access routes that are made delightful with a nature interlude.

Windows at the courtyard side and the front garden side of the home create air channels that ensure natural air flow in the home, which keeps the environment comfortable, even in the scorching Nagoya summer. The front-facing window enjoys a scenery of fluttering leaves that dance on tree branches, oblivious to worries, just as how life next to nature usually is.

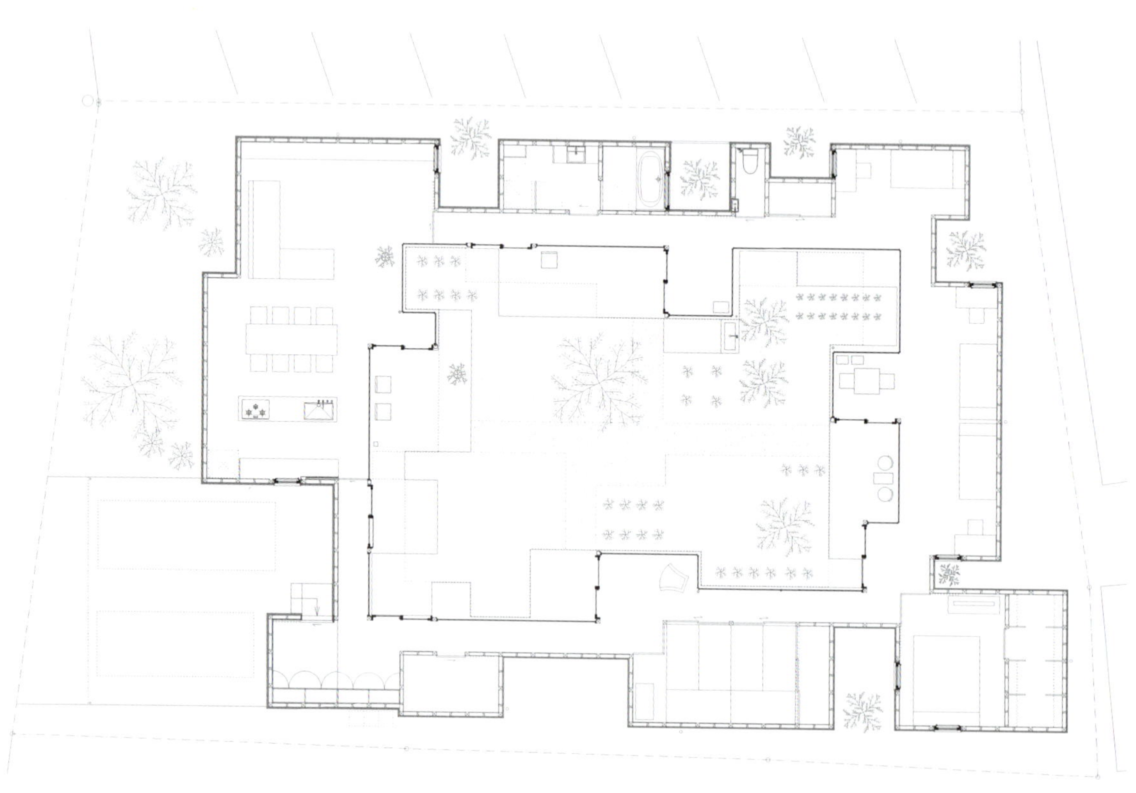

FLOOR PLAN

SECTIONS

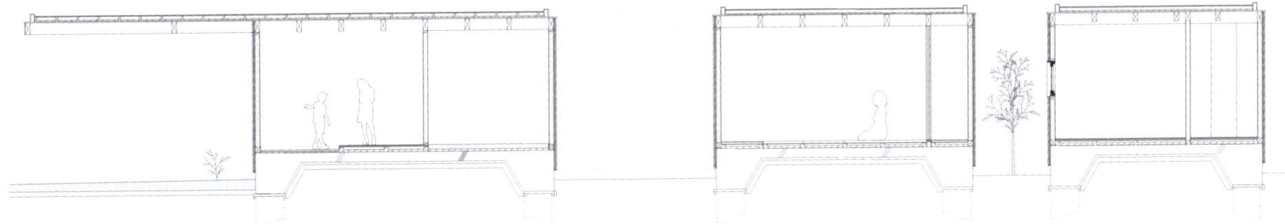

Location /
Obu city, Aichi Prefecture, Japan

Area /
1,302 square feet (121 square meters)

Completion /
2018

Design /
1-1 Architects, ENZO. Co., Ltd

Photography /
1-1 Architects

House YO

History meets modern

This 50-year-old home, first built as a guesthouse to the main house on the site, is tailored for the modern-day life of a couple and their children. The home's close proximity to the main house (still present and inhabited) places it in view of curious gazes, challenging privacy; a reinforced-concrete structure also provides little room for architectural changes without compromising the structural system. Limiting design work to the interior and outside, the house retains its original structure (as requested by the residents), and by way of that, the heritage of the home that has been passed down from generation to generation. An updated privacy-friendly exterior accommodates the family's modern lifestyle, while also allowing them the freedom to enjoy their home without the worry of being watched. It is complemented with a modern, dry garden that intermingles greenery with rock boulders to erect symbolisms of natural mountains.

The unusually large window and door openings are embraced and pronounced to create opportunities to appreciate the scenery: L-shaped

LUCKY PLAZA

hollows created by the uncoordinated fit between modern fittings and the existing skeletal structure are creatively utilized to extend their functional quality as decking (*engawa*) and rain shelter under extended eaves.

In the garden, boulder placements and greenery are integrated with strategically placed viewpoints through a clever division of space. As anchoring elements, the boulders add impact and make a bold statement. A cherry blossom heightens the "drama," captivating attention with pink blooms that add a burst of color to the green in the space. Rectangular slabs pave a path that leads from the main entrance, through the garden, to a raised perch, from where one can drink in the view in its entirety. Along the way, a tree pruned to appear like clouds adds variety and dimension to the garden scape. The garden scenery seeps into the home through windows on both the first and second floor, completing moments in the home with pleasing, restorative views.

FIRST-FLOOR PLAN

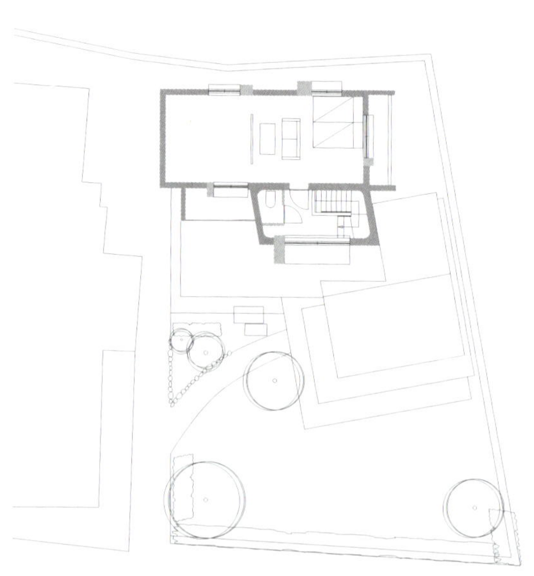

SECOND-FLOOR PLAN

Location /
Tokyo, Japan

Area /
980 square feet (91 square meters)

Completion /
2010

Design /
Takeshi Hosaka Architects

Photography /
Koji Fuji (Nacasa & Partners Inc.)

Inside Out

Inviting the "out" in

Home to a married couple and two cats, the house, located in Tokyo, is inspired along the idea that the humans and cats live in the same house, instead of the cats living in a house designed for humans. This shaped into the design concept, "a house in which being inside feels like you are outside."

The building is shaped as an irregular rectangle to match the shape of the site. A sealable internal volume sits within an external volume that welcomes the elements through integrated openings in the roof and walls, purposefully designed for light, wind, and rain to enter the home. The living and dining area are contained behind sliding glass doors in the internal volume, while the bedroom and bathroom are placed in the external volume.

Planned spaces that experience the mood of the elements outside create the ambiance of being outside, while resting comfortably at home. The daily way of life in this home is weather-dependant and the unique design of the home creates a variety of living choices within a single day.

The openings in the walls and roof connect visually to the outdoor while also bringing the elements in.The openings in the roof are aligned above small tree plots dug into the earth so that they are watered naturally by rain. Arranged throughout the outer volume, these plots present like micro courtyards that fill the home with natural greenery. Watching the leaves shiver in the wind, or feeling the splatter of the rain as it hits the

tree branches enhances the "outside-in" experience of feeling like one is outside, while being inside at home.

Experiencing the feel of the rain, the kiss of the sun, and the brush of the breeze right at home makes for an interesting and joyful lifestyle, especially in figuring out ideal spots to catch the breeze, or to enjoy the cool of the rain in a storm without furniture getting drenched. The cats too join in the fun of living with the elements, basking in their favorite sunny spots and determining the best routes to avoid wet paws when a drizzle is pitter-pattering.

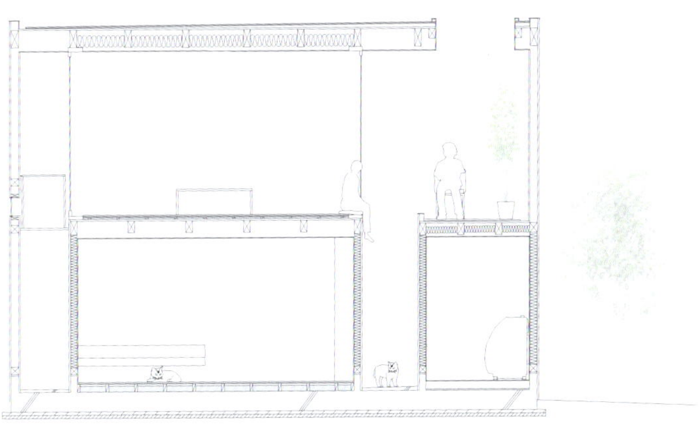

SECTION

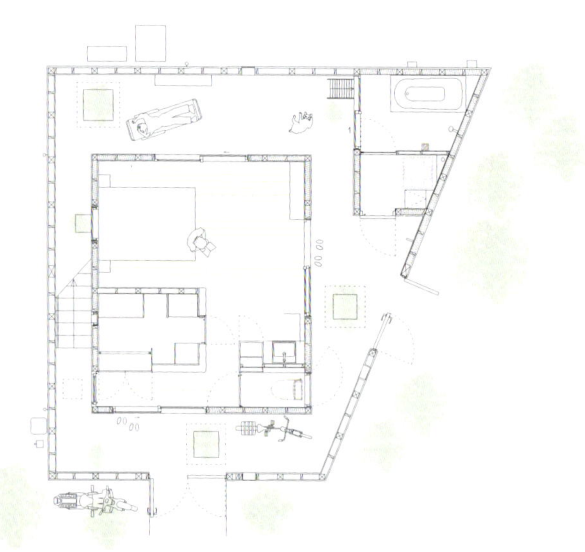

FIRST-FLOOR PLAN

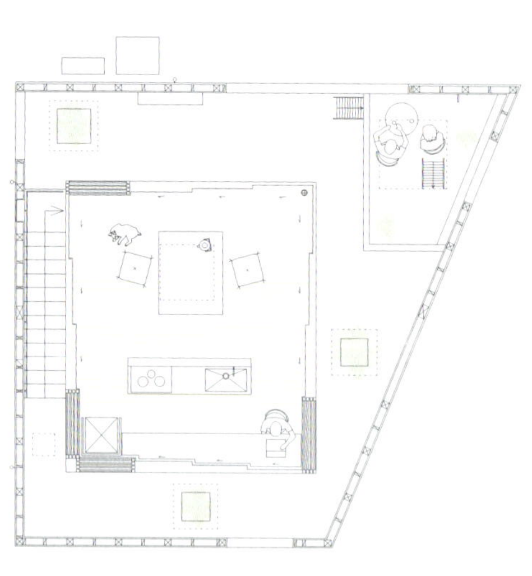

SECOND-FLOOR PLAN

WAIKIKI
AUSTIN POWERS

Location /
Shiga, Japan

Area /
1,249 square feet (116 square meters)

Completion /
2017

Design /
Hearth Architects

Photography /
Yuta Yamada

Shoei House

Nurturing nature inside and out

This small house, with a footprint measuring 18 feet (5.5 meters) in width and 105 feet (32 meters) in depth, is built in the traditional house style of Kyoto known as "*unagi no nedoko*," or "bedding of an eel," given its long form. Enclosed by buildings to the left and right, the home receives limited natural light and fresh air. The main living areas, such as the living and dining room and kitchen are arranged on the second floor that is raised on pilotis; the first floor houses the bedrooms and a bathroom. Skylights and windows invite natural light in to brighten up the home, which would otherwise contend with a dim interior. An opening carved into the second floor helps illuminate the home, but more importantly, it considers space for the rubber tree in the ground below to grow without restrictions, allowing it to stretch its woody limbs in glorious existence. This rubber tree is joined by other greenery scattered around inside and outside the home, such

as the Ryubin Thai fern planted in a trough set in the kitchen cabinetry, prioritizing the inclusion of nature within the home. The endearing table-top garden is arranged like a Japanese garden, with pebbles and rocks, and lifts the décor by adding a splash of vibrant greenery that complements the timber-focused space. The garden outside combines deciduous trees, such as Aodamo (Japanese ash) and Negishi (Japanese white pine) obtained from the Gifu mountains. Landscaped with native plants, moss and rocks, the pleasant Japanese-style garden embraces the home in a peaceful aura. As time passes, the change of the seasons reflects in the garden and trees to create an engaging environment for the residents to appreciate nature's resplendence and enjoy the simple pleasures of life.

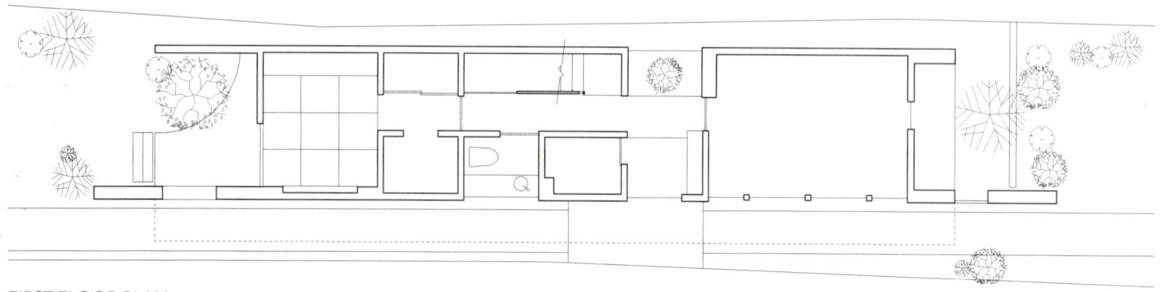

FIRST-FLOOR PLAN

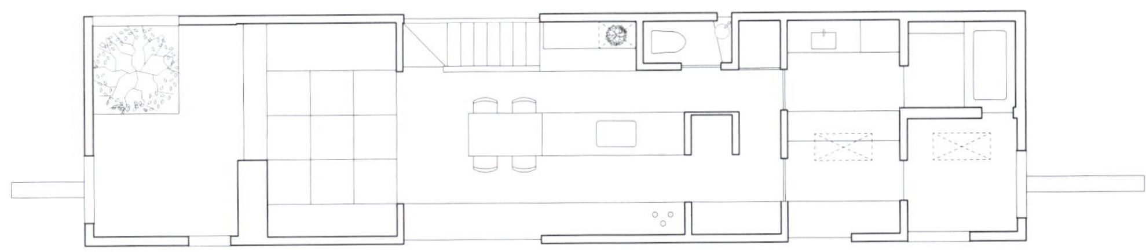

SECOND-FLOOR PLAN

Location /
Yokohama city, Kanagawa, Japan

Area /
3,305 square feet (307 square meters)

Completion /
2017

Design /
Takeshi Hosaka Architects

Photography /
Koji Fuji (Nacasa & Partners Inc.)

House in Kozukue

Wide spaces and courtyards

Set on top of the small mountain in Shin-Yokohama, this home shares its building site with a parking lot that once took up the entire area. To manage its overly "lively" surroundings of car headlights, exhaust fumes, people's voices, and the various "concertos" of the nearby vending machine dispensing purchases, the home is closed as much as possible, with small windows and a single door.

The interior contradicts the sealed exterior with an airy open layout that prides itself on space excesses that are sometimes unnecessary, but favored, so as to create a sense of expanse and generosity in the layout; it also serves the homeowners in hosting special gatherings.

To that extent, a common room features in the interior together with multiple semi-outdoor spaces that take up a good half of the plan. These semi-outdoor courtyards fill the home with natural light and ventilation, while doubling as leisure spaces for the family and their guests. Composing small dry gardens and rock gardens, these courtyards present contemporary reflections of a typical Japanese garden. They also successfully cross the borders of indoor and outdoor, blending both space definitions to create a connected, minimalist home that pays homage to the cultural tradition of a *tsuboniwa* in the home.

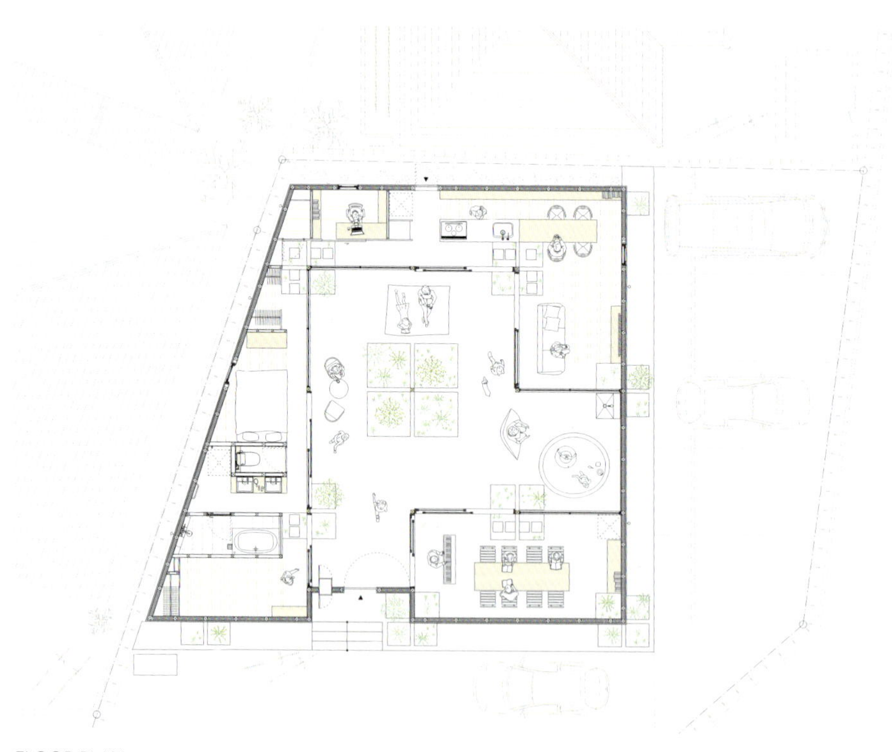

FLOOR PLAN

Location /
Shiga Prefecture, Japan

Area /
4,855 square feet (451 square meters)

Completion /
2019

Design /
Masaru Takahashi Architectural Design Office

Photographer /
Nao Takahashi

House Near Shigarakigu

A U-shaped garden access

This wooden, one-story courthouse in Shiga Prefecture considers a new way of living, set in an open site that is almost on par with the road level. Selected for its barrier-free compound, the site willingly adheres to the one-story plan that wraps around a central courtyard. Designed in this way, the home fluidly integrates the outdoor into daily life, while also giving room for privacy. In this U-shaped layout, the spaces flow in a continuous change along a path of public and private zones.

The courtyard garden can conveniently be accessed from each zone independently to preserve privacy in the areas within the home. A neighbor who pops by for a chat can be led into the calm garden from the porch without intruding on the inner living spaces. Similarly, the living area and the bedrooms each have their own garden access, allowing a quiet reprieve in the garden without having to disrupt the activities in the other areas of the home. Glass doors that face the courtyard in the living and dining area and bedrooms lend the garden's scenery to the spaces; they also fill the home with natural light. In the guestroom, horizontal glass panels at the bottom of the garden wall present a view of the *tsukubai* (water basin) and the plants around it. Translating the traditions of the *tsuboniwa*, the courtyard is set simply, with a small selection of greenery, swept in an expanse of gravel-filled space. An L-shaped deck extends out from the home into the garden, partly under eaves, providing shelter in all climates to immerse in the serenity of the garden.

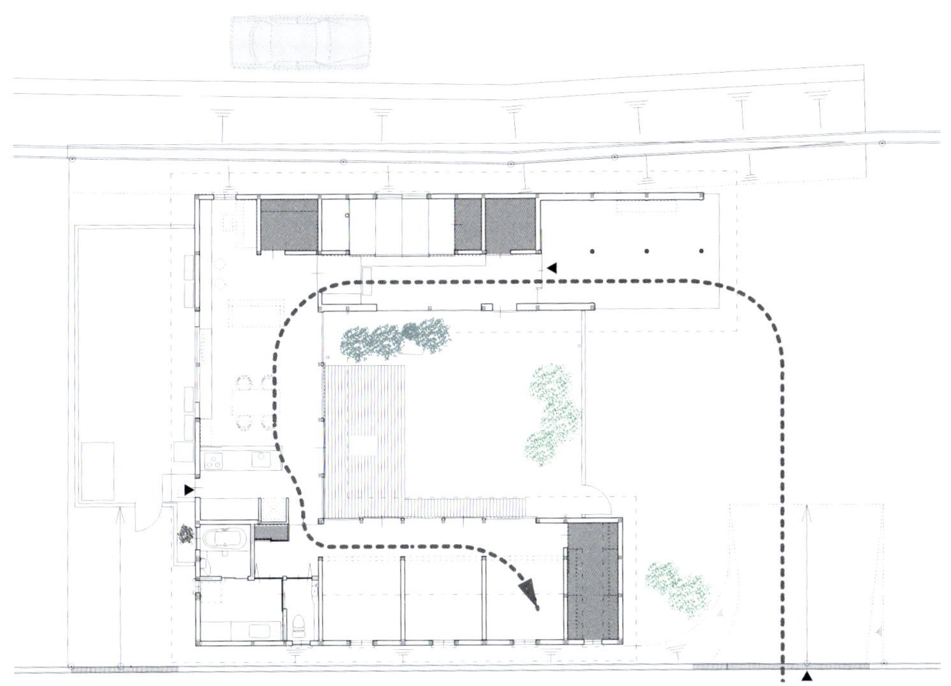

FLOOR PLAN

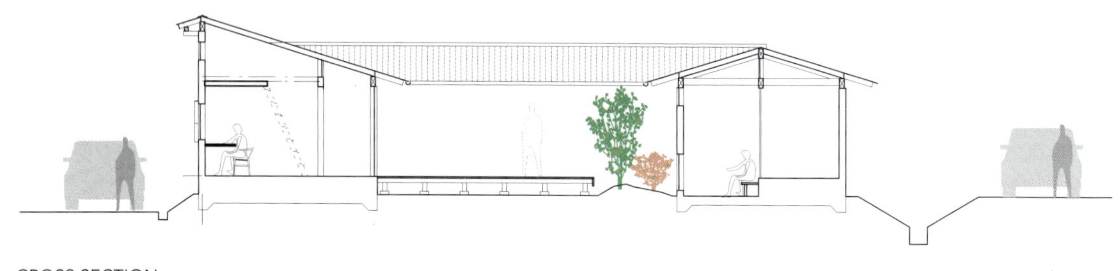

CROSS SECTION

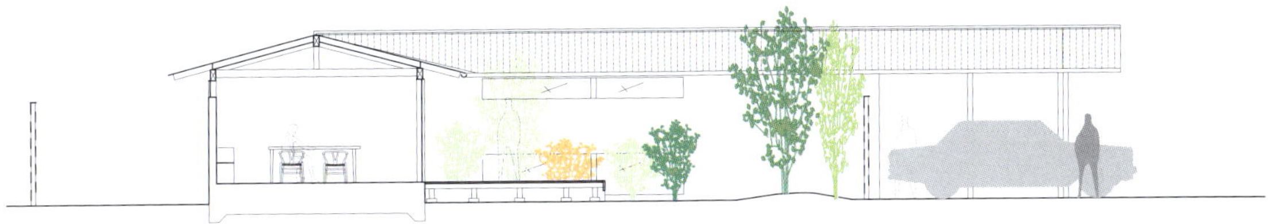

LONG SECTION

Location /
Osaka, Japan

Area /
1,195 square feet (111 square meters)

Completion /
2018

Design /
SPACESPACE

Photography /
Koichi Torimura

Mushroom House

Making room and garden for life

At the foot of a mountain range in Kawachinagano, a city in Osaka Prefecture, this two-story wooden home is ensconced by old senior dwelling, which form the area's traditional townscape. Designed for a dual-career couple, the home seeks to amplify the joys of life during the couple's time intersections, such as breakfast together and days off work. An outdoor garden and a tatami room provide inviting spaces for relaxation and time together in a Y-shaped floor plan that is configured to accommodate the pleasant views, the sun cycle, and specifically, city infrastructures, such as the telegraph pole at the site boundary.

To prevent the marring of the façade, the house volume bifurcates at the telegraph pole, making for an eye-catching design that also creates more defined spaces to elaborate a variety of lifestyles for the couple's quality time with each other. Primary living areas, including the kitchen and dining room are located on the first floor, with bedrooms on the second, accessed by stairs.

Food being the center of life in this home, the garden transcends mere aesthetics to also supply menu ingredients such as herbs and fruits from the trees. A rammed-earth verge traces the garden boundary, creating corner pockets that can be used as flower beds, or to plant seasonal crop. It is also a rustic garden bench that invites the couple to extend their activities outdoor.

The earth border leads to a set of stone stairs that double as a perch from where one can engage in a peaceful commune with nature. The stairs ascend to the roof of the adjoining tatami room—another inviting spot that allows opportunities to get creative with outdoor family time next to nature. A short ladder leads the circulation from the roof to back indoors, accessing the bedroom on the second floor. The tatami room overlooks the garden and weaves in another level of nature appreciation as one unclutters the mind to immerse in the reviving energy of the garden beyond.

止まれ

FLOOR PLAN

SECTION

Location /
Nagoya, Aichi, Japan

Area /
1,152 square feet (107 square meters)

Completion /
2016

Design /
studio velocity

Photography /
studio velocity

6 Roofs House

Roofs over gardens

Interspersed with vibrant courtyards and gardens throughout, this home forms under six HP (hyperbolic paraboloid) shell roofs arranged in a sloping, overlapping configuration to reflect the undulating topography of the area. The roofs are set in varying heights, with eaves angled higher at the center of the site and tilting lower toward the perimeter. A sloping gradient traces the roof line, channeling the flow of rainwater with ease; gaps in the overlapping areas allow natural elements, such as wind and light to pass, creating a continuity between the inside and outside.

Elaborating this cohesion of the interior and exterior are cheerful gardens that are scattered around the home. Almost every living space is hedged with a pocket of greenery that adds plenty of green cheer to the interior. A lane of gravel verges the garden, symbolizing the calming flow of a stream, tying back to the element of water in a traditional *niwa*. Floor-to-ceiling glass walls proffer these garden sceneries and flood the interior with ample natural light. Imbued with

the uplifting vibe of trees and greenery, the home reflects an appreciation and respect for nature deeply-rooted in the Japanese culture. Days are passed in pleasant appreciation of sunlight glinting off leaves and shadows of tree canopies dancing on lawns.

The home's exterior greenery rolls out to connect to adjacent streets along its entire perimeter, unlike other houses in the neighborhood that come off as aloof and shut-in, surrounded by walls all around. This unusual, open landscaping is inviting and creates a park-like home that helps bridge distances in the community, presenting an open invitation for a friendly greet-and-chat with neighbors who pass.

FLOOR PLAN

SECTION

Location /
Okazaki city, Japan

Area /
2,691 square feet (250 square meters)

Completion /
2016

Design /
studio velocity

Photography /
Shinkenchiku-sha Photo Department

House in Yanagibata

Divided connection

This home and private hairdressing salon fits itself into a colorful mix that includes a dense residential development, a paddy field, a bus stop, and a string of public/community buildings. Arranged as a cluster of twenty-six dispersed volumes, the home makes room for community engagement through a porous environment that involves itself in its surroundings: a community space to its north, a garden that trails through the site—often used by children to get to and from piano classes nearby, and a canopied wait area around the municipal bus stop at the front of the home for commuters (who could potentially become customers of the salon).

The diagonal garden that extends through the site from south to east also separates the residential space from the hairdresser studio, which is set closer to the street and public access. The residential units, set further from the intersection, are organized in a continuous flow that incorporates a living room, bedrooms, kitchen, bathroom, and a library.

いしかわ内科
クリニック
ココ

This fragmented, splayed organization of the volumes relieves the heaviness of the dense backdrop of residential developments, while promoting fluid mobility. In distorting the home's physical boundaries, the design incorporates pockets of space that are transformed into courtyards that inject vibrance and life to the home and neighborhood, playing off the adjacent sea of green that is the paddy field. Planted with bushes and trees, the courtyards embrace the home with nature through repeated visual integration with the interior, aided by glass doors and high ceilings. Every turn glimpses a reviving view of evergreen and deciduous trees that create rich, red and golden portraits come fall. The combination of the home's white exterior and the greenery, lovingly tended to and nurtured by the resident's grandfather, create an attractive tapestry that spruces up the somber neighborhood with its canopy of gray roofs.

FLOOR PLAN

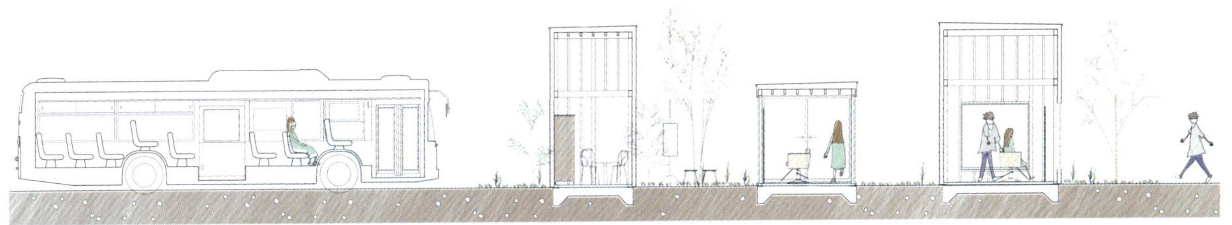

SECTION

Location /
Kamakura, Kanagawa, Japan

Area /
1,647 square feet (153 square meters)

Completion /
2019

Design /
G Architects Studio

Photography /
Daisuke Shima

Small Houses for Ryokan

The sea, a *ryokan*, and a garden

This small house is in fact two houses: one a residence for the owners, and the other, a *ryokan*, which is a traditional Japanese inn that accommodates guests. Divided into a main house and an annex, the home is situated in a dense residential area and faces the sea on its short side. The first floor of the main building is a dining room nestled by the garden on one side and the ocean on another, bestowing views for every mood and occasion. The second floor is dedicated as the owners' residence; it is modestly sized in comparison to other areas so as to enhance guest spaces. The *ryokan* is rented out as a whole building unit so guests can enjoy solitude and privacy with little intrusions.

The space between the two volumes is filled out with a serene garden that is accessed by stepping stones that lead through a lush, feathery lawn. The path ends at a *sensui* (a body of water) that circles a small peninsula (*dejima*), which extends out from the lawn. An *ishidoro* (stone lantern) decorates the *dejima,* placed in full view as one of the garden's primary showpiece. The composition is completed with symbolic rock arrangements that unite these traditional Japanese garden elements in a picture of calming simplicity. As the eyes take in each piece in detail, the view is gently ushered beyond the *niwa* to the dining area and the sliver of the ocean framed scenically within its window, urging one to contemplate the quiet beauty of nature.

SITE PLAN

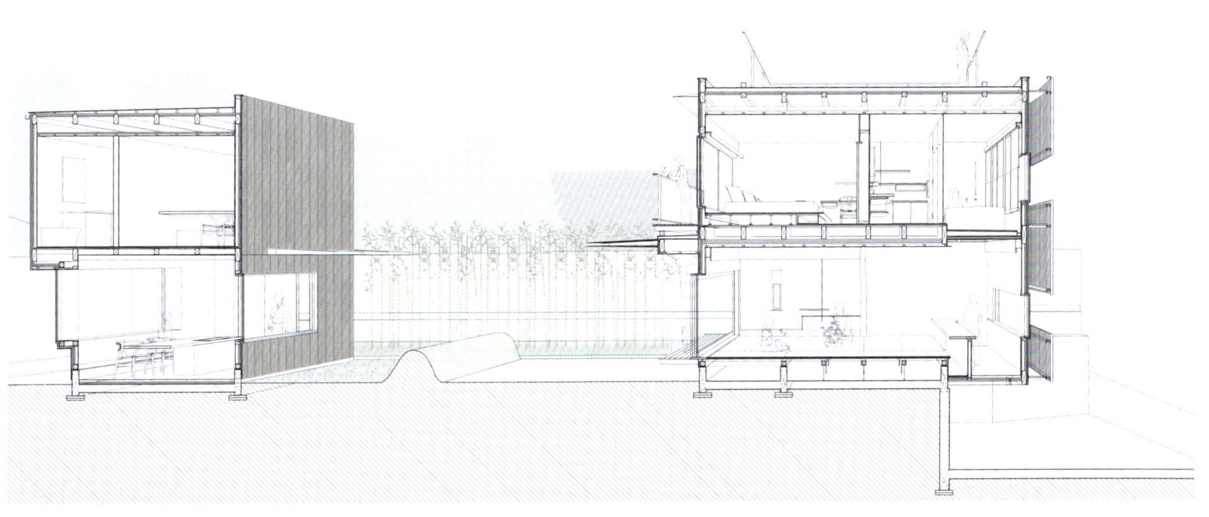

SECTION

Location /
Hyogo Prefecture, Japan

Area /
1,711 square feet (159 square meters)

Completion /
2018

Design /
Tomohiro Hata Architect and Associates

Photography /
Toshiyuki Yano

Loop Terrace

All-around viewpoint and connection

With a concrete base and a white metal façade, this home, situated against a densely packed neighborhood of muted, concrete exteriors, gleams like a bright jewel. To negate the visually noisy surroundings, a central courtyard garden springs from the heart of the home, filling it with a lightness that contrasts the crowded scenery outside; it also installs a sanctuary of serenity with trees and rock arrangements.

Inspired by the Katsura Imperial Villa, an important cultural icon of Japan, the home references its structure and elements of delight in a compact iteration that threads a keen relationship between indoor and outdoor throughout. Spaces flow in a loop around a soothing courtyard garden, linked to it by a series of terraces that interpret the traditional Japanese *engawa* (elevated verandas) in typical Japanese homes; this terraced design takes inspiration from the Katsura Villa with its *engawa* overlooking the garden.

The building structure that circles the courtyard is specifically configured to be one-room deep, ensuring that all the spaces in the home have a connection to the tranquil nature—either through windows, floor-to-ceiling openings, or the terraces, which sometimes extend under eaves, so the scenery can be enjoyed even through the elements. The two-floor plan is connected by white staircases that mimic the clean color palette of the building, alongside a décor of light wood. Through a play of levels orchestrated by connecting staircases and terraces, the home enjoys varying sightlines that enhance its unique character.

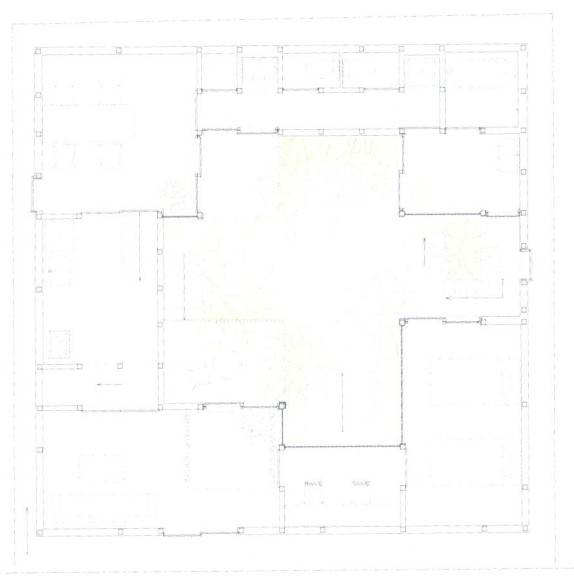

FIRST-FLOOR PLAN

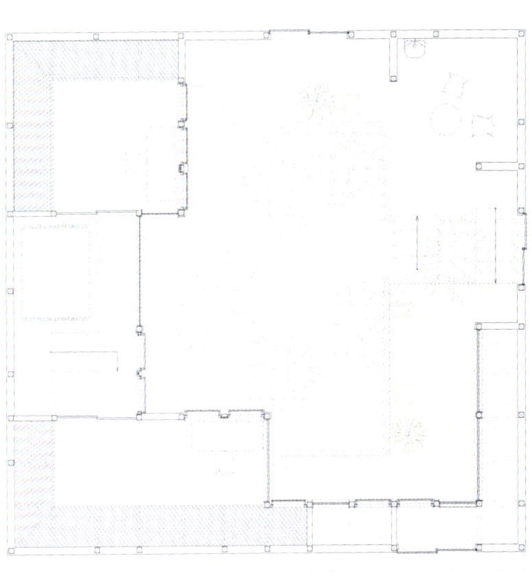

SECOND-FLOOR PLAN

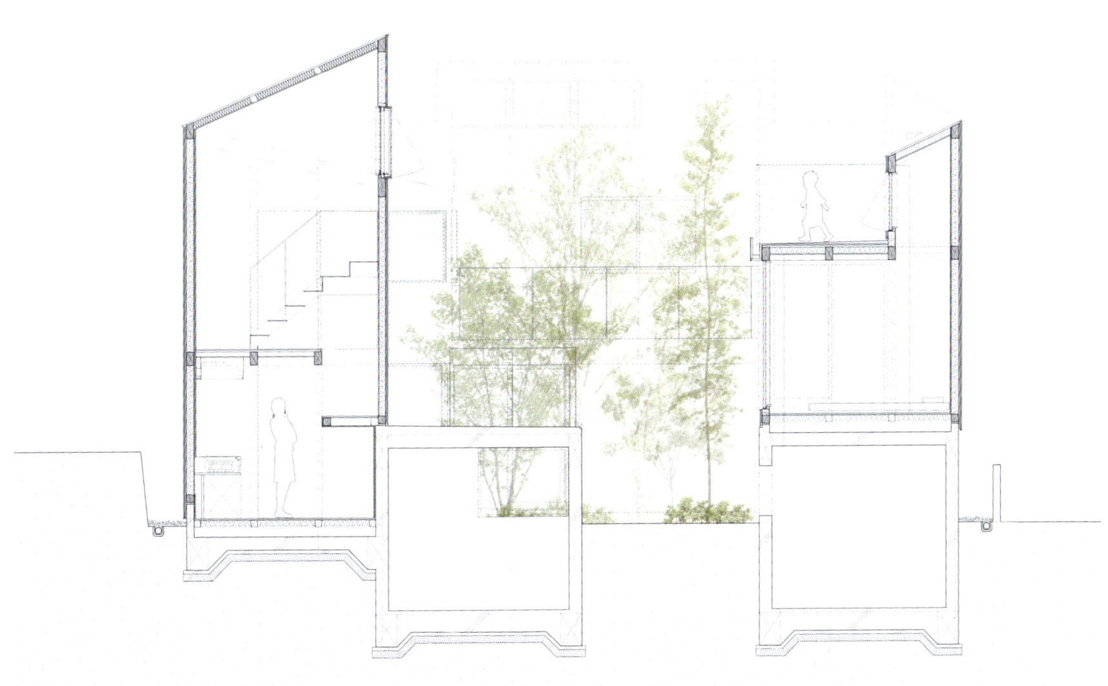

SECTION

Location /
Okinawa, Japan

Area /
1,453 square feet (135 square meters)

Completion /
2019

Design /
Studio Monaka

Photography /
Kazuoki Yasugi

House OM

A modern twist on tradition

Nestled 23 feet (7 meters) below street level, this home in Okinawa is the result of careful consideration to control its visibility and protect privacy, being at the bottom of a slope. An open design, receptive to the Okinawan elements, yet strong enough to withstand their destructive tantrums, organizes two adjacent volumes—with one specifically housing all the areas that require plumbing. This is in response to drainpipes located 5 feet (1.5 meters) above ground level, requiring the bathroom and the toilet to be set higher than other rooms.

The living area volume designs a U-shaped walkway that recalls an *amahaji* (an open corridor that borders the outside of a house), doing away with a formal front door. Therefore, shoes are removed only when entering individual interior areas, instead of at the "front door," as is customary. This layout steps away from convention—as requested by the homeowners—and creates a relaxed resort feel in the home.

However, tradition still completes the design as the *amahaji* encloses a peaceful courtyard, stretching out under a U-shaped eave to create areas to reflect and ponder quietly beside nature. The smattering of greenery also livens the sullen, concrete backdrop and refreshes the ambiance with nature, proffered to the interior spaces through large glass doors. More greenery accompanies the home with

a strip of garden that runs between the two building structures. Lined with gravel and tree planters, this passage of Zen is symbolic of a stream flowing past the home as it imparts a calm energy to the open-concept living and dining room and aligns the access to the garage and the outside.

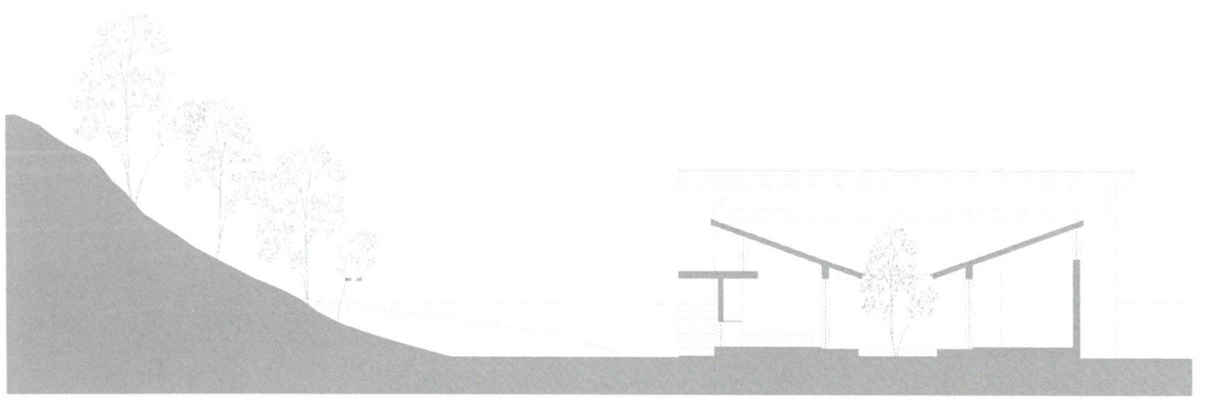

SECTION

Location /
Matsumoto city, Japan

Area /
5,059 square feet (470 square meters)

Completion /
2017

Design /
CUBO design architect

Photography /
Koichi Torimura

M4

Chasing views and mountains

This residence overlooks the city of Matsumoto and the beautiful mountain ridgeline beyond. Windows in varying sizes, heights, shapes, and designs frame sweeping views that offer transient portraits painted by the changing hues of the sky, the drift of the clouds, the cycle of seasons, and even the evolving character of the mountains. Seeming like random afterthoughts in the home's aesthetic consideration, the windows are in fact meticulously set to present a diverse and dynamic sequence of scenes from every nook and every level of the interior, so that a beautiful scenery always accompanies one, whether sitting or standing. They are, however, limited to the back of the home, so natural light enters exclusively from one direction, increasing lighting and shadow contrasts that are heightened by the barnacle-inspired design of the striking bay windows.

The V-shape of the site extends the generosity of the view, pairing activities within the home with a backdrop of the cityscape and the misty undulations of the mountain peaks, which also serve as "borrowed scenery," or *shakkei* for the vibrant backyard garden. Accessed via steps that connect to a small back porch, the garden begins with stepping-stones that disperse into a graveled path. The end of the path presents the feature tree, which gives the garden a central focus. Expanses of lawn, rock placements and gravel elements (in the background and mid-ground) complete the garden's deliberate arrangement to create a sense of spaciousness that encourages body, mind, and soul to relax. A sheltered deck iterates a traditional *engawa* (veranda) and skirts the back perimeter to create ample viewpoints for enjoying the peaceful calm of nature.

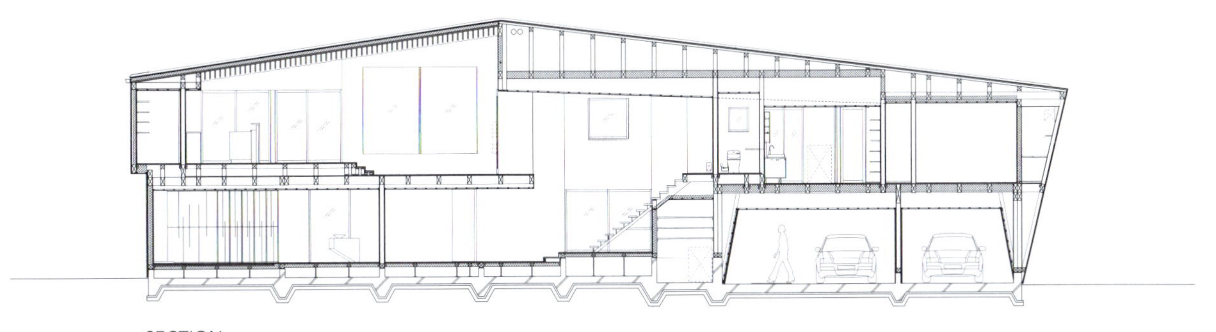

SECTION

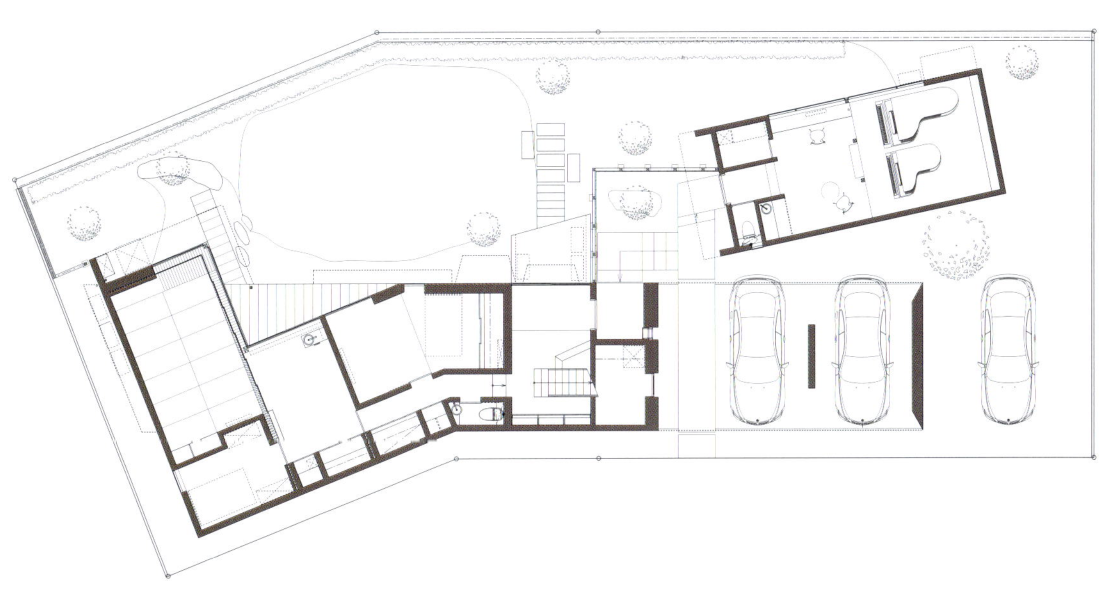

FIRST-FLOOR PLAN

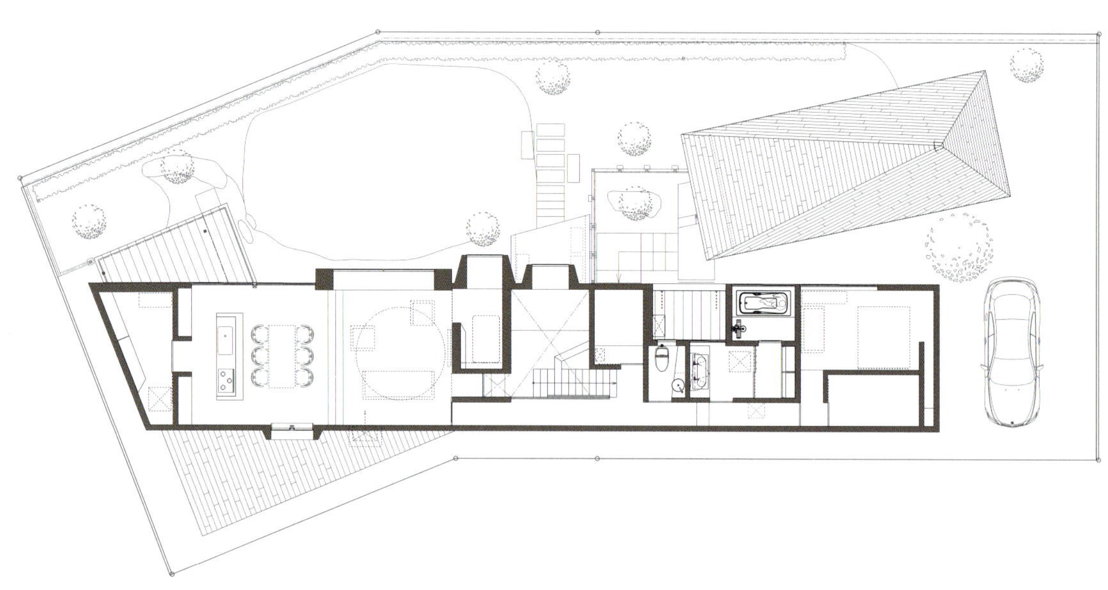

SECOND-FLOOR PLAN

Location /
Osaka, Japan

Area /
1,410 square feet (131 square meters)

Completion /
2017

Design /
SAI Architectural Design Office

Photography /
Norihito Yamauchi

Melt House

Growing together with nature

The indoor courtyard garden in this home—one of its most commanding feature—is the creative inspiration that shapes the home's plan. The residents sought a home that would connect them to nature as they carried out their day-to-day—not just via views through a glass pane, but also through the senses, as life takes place around this nature. The courtyard garden meets this design request, forming the anchor of the home's design.

Set in a narrow site in a residential area, the home is organized within buildings in the north and south corners of the site's linear layout. The space between the two volumes is roofed and transformed into an indoor courtyard garden that involves itself in the activities of the family. The scent of the bark; the rustling of the leaves; the sparkle of dew on the foliage, and other such characteristics of nature become interwoven with daily life. The dry garden, composed in rock arrangements, pebbles, gravel, and trees showcase a composition adhered to creating a soothing environment that benefits well-being. The seasons are experienced through deciduous trees that shed their leaves, and the elements through the double-height, partially-opened volume of the space, which ushers in cool winds in the winter, the light spray of the rain in spring, and streaming sun rays in the summer. Light also finds its way in through clerestory windows that fill the home with plenty of natural light despite its linear plan.

The spaces in the home are arranged on either side of the garden within two wings. One houses the kitchen and dining room, and bedrooms on the second floor, while the other, the living room, a traditional Japanese room (almost like a modern interpretation of a tatami room), and a second-floor loft. This home goes the distance to prove that even within a small area, one can exist with nature as a part of life, both growing together in a unique space.

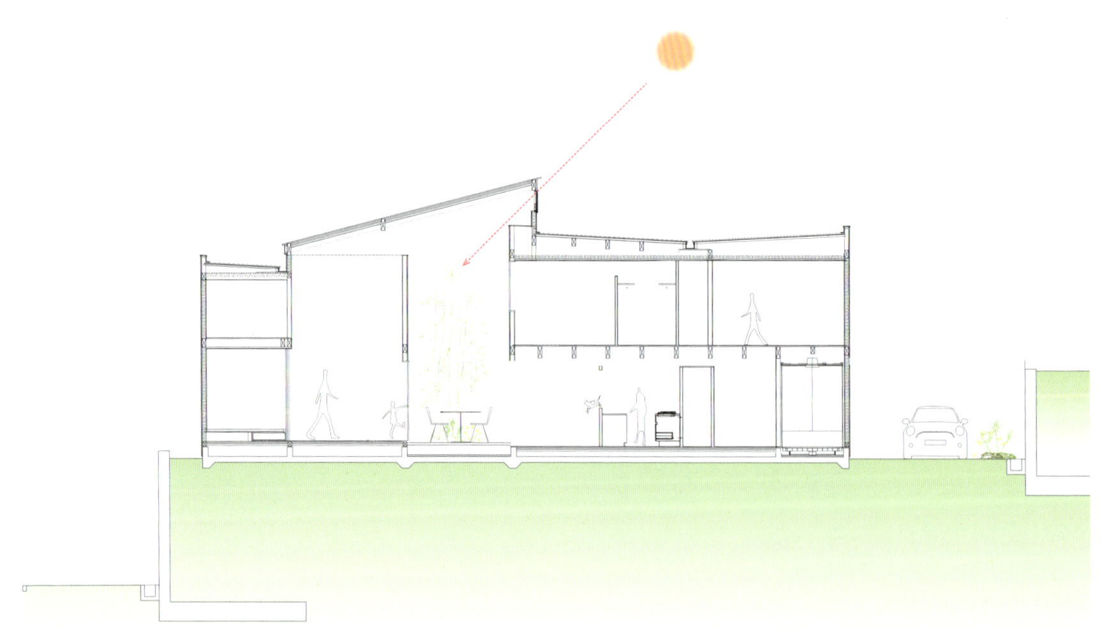

SECTION

Location /
Hamamatsu, Japan

Area /
1,356 square feet (126 square meters)

Completion /
2016

Design /
Arii Irie Architects

Photography /
Daici Ano

House with Gardens and Roofs

Flowing spaces that create time-trusted connections

Located in Hamamatsu, a city on the southern coast of Central Japan, this home is no stranger to a warm climate. An elevated roof on support beams over prime living spaces pursues ventilation and air flow, while creating the impression of an airy outdoor space to manage the stifling climate of the region.

A detached extension of an existing house built in 1983, the home is formed by linear volumes that stretch over the site to incorporate a courtyard and pockets of integrated garden space. Sliding doors and windows open to connect the home with the outdoor, creating a welcoming and peaceful ambiance. A deck that extends west along the courtyard presents an ideal outdoor section for evening recreations and gatherings with friends, while watching the sky blush as the sun kisses it goodnight.

The interior is a network of flowing spaces composed with contrasting dark and light timber, adding dynamism to the linear layout. As passages turn and hallways divert, living spaces are revealed, or uncovered behind doors. Essentials concealed behind a sweep of storage keeps lines clean and interior aesthetics free of jarring intrusions, as the large openings in the façade nuance the natural décor further with views of the surrounding evergreens. A beautiful dining table carved from wood completes the organic palette of the interior and gathers the family together for memorable mealtimes in the soothing surrounds of nature.

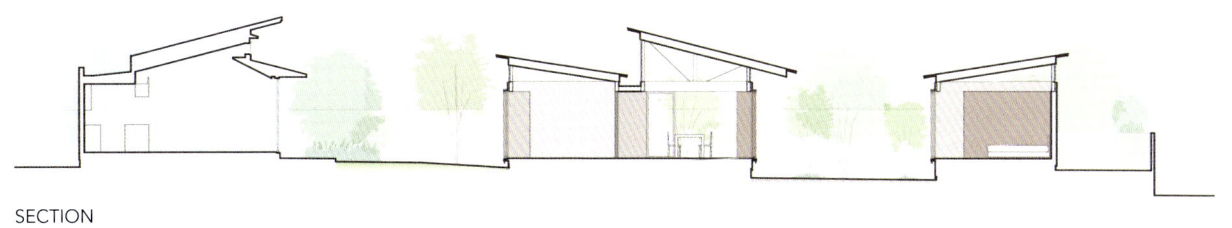

SECTION

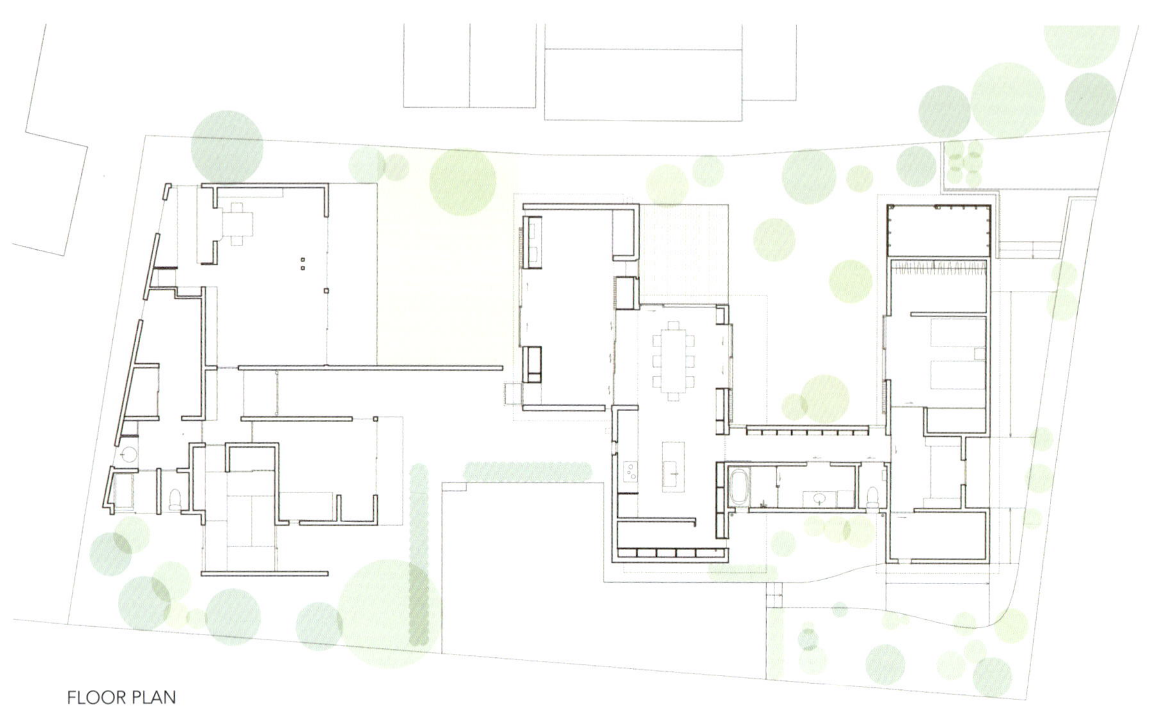

FLOOR PLAN

Location /
Kyoto, Japan

Area /
2,465 square feet (229 square meters)

Completion /
2016

Design /
Alphaville Architects

Photography /
Yasutake Kondo

Gable Roof House

Twisting the perspective for great views

This contemporary home that overlooks green spaces from every possible angle interprets the traditional gable roof with a "twist," to fill the home with reviving scenes of nature. Spanning a deep plot, the original roof had composed a stark, stretched axis that distributed sunlight unevenly and challenged the roof design with outward thrust. To rectify that, the redesign divides the roof into four parts, creating room to realign and resize (in height) the home's volumes, as well as integrate enveloping pockets of garden around the outside of the home.

The center of the home, a single-story volume housing the kitchen and dining area is rotated at a 30-degree angle and installed with glass walls that look out to the garden from different angles. Unlike conventional Japanese courtyards, these reinterpreted green spaces borrow the external scenery in their composition to enhance the appreciation of these capsules of nature. A combination of trees, perennials, and lawn spaces create green respites that offer much-needed opportunities for solitude in today's modern lifestyle, to recharge and realign. Visible from main living areas, the gardens, cast in sun rays, lift the ambiance of the home and always present vibrant and uplifting views to set the eyes on.

The jagged sequence of rooms and varying roof heights—a welcome consequence of combining single and double-storied volumes with a "twist"—create a sense of openness within the home that ties in well with the relaxing outdoor sceneries that permeate throughout. These tranquil garden connections add depth and define a home to truly delight in.

EXPLODED AXONOMETRIC DIAGRAM

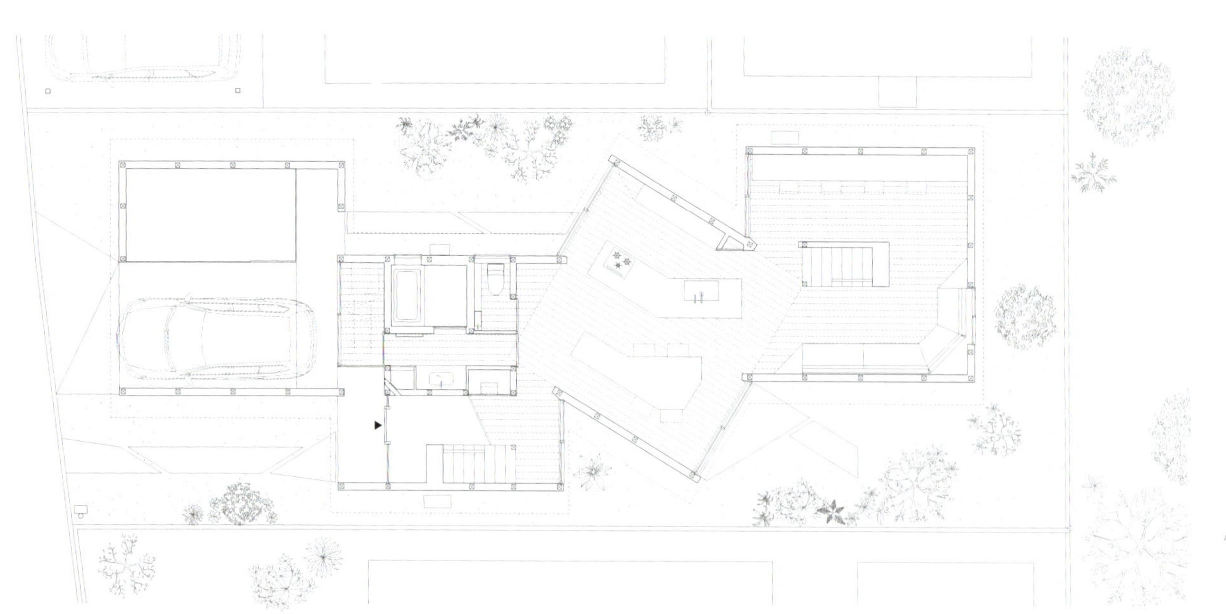

FIRST-FLOOR PLAN

Location /
Osaka, Japan

Area /
775 square feet (72 square meters)

Completion /
2019

Design /
arbol

Photography /
Yasunori Shimomura

House in Kawachinagano

Going with the flow

The scenery that meets this house in Kawachinagano city, Osaka, is idyllic, sketched with a gurgling river and misty mountain peaks. To draw the most out of the surroundings, the home is designed to experience all facets of the site's beauty and allure.

Set beside the Amami river that streams down from Kisen Mountain, the house organizes itself in a linear program that "flows with the current," enhancing the presence of the splashing stream as one moves about and uses the spaces in the home. Past the entrance, an integrated living–dining room acts as a viewing gallery, overlooking the rippling mountains in the distant and the nearby river verged by lush greenery. Foggy peaks and valleys mark a wavy ridge that reflects the flowing movement of the water to paint a matching backdrop that is entrancing.

A backyard garden brings nature closer to home and is enjoyed with little restrictions from an *engawa* (veranda)—composed as a wooden deck at the back of the home—that offers an ideal spot to put feet up and relax outdoor beside the hush of greenery. Lending the therapeutic qualities of nature to daily activities, the garden extends the length of the home and brinks the bedroom and home entrance. As branches sway and leaves rustle, a calm descends; tense nerves are reset and mental alignment is accessed. The healing hands of nature have been known to work wonders and here, by the river, their power is twofold, as the home draws soothing connections to both greenery and the element of water, in some way recalling the set-up of a traditional *niwa* (garden) with a *chisen* (pond).

White painted walls create an airy quality in the small plan, as a steep, mono-pitch roof draws in natural daylight. The easy ambiance is harmonized with a selective furniture collection that highlights the beauty of the natural surroundings; in this home that welcomes nature as willingly as it is a part of it, life pursues completeness and contentment.

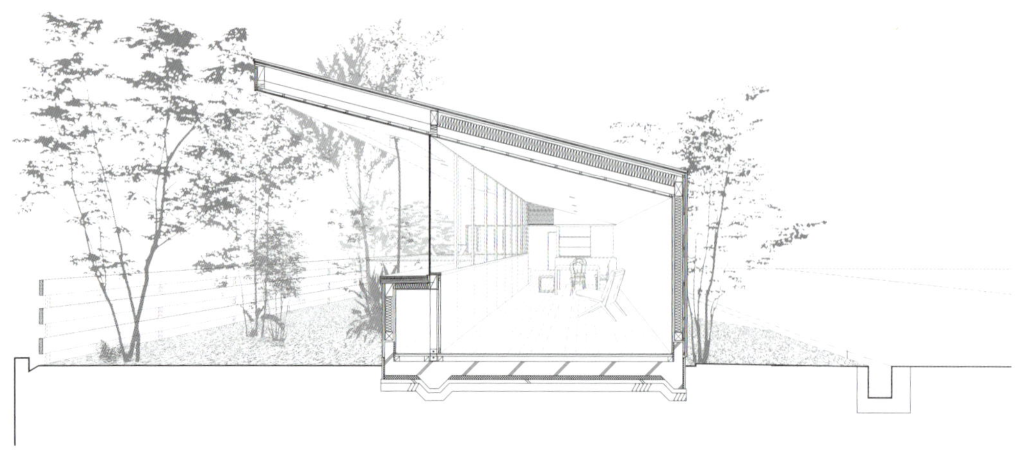

SECTION

Location /
Tokyo, Japan

Area /
1,292 square feet (120 square meters)

Completion /
2016

Design /
frontofficetokyo

Photography /
Takumi Ota

Oyamadai House

Ground and garden as one

In a dense city where the practice is to retreat behind walls to relish privacy, this house, surrounded by neighbors on all four sides, keeps life open. Why? Because everybody else is sealed in shut.

Taking advantage of the architectural landscape of its surroundings, this home pursues an open plan without compromising privacy, as neighboring houses are closed in within walls to stay out of view. So, over two floors, wrapped entirely in glazing, this home organizes an exposed lifestyle that is, ironically, also private.

Each floor is designed as a single room, with personal and private spaces like bedrooms and the facilities organized within "boxes."

The second floor, which locates the living room, is set at 10 feet (3 meters) from the ground to take in the view of the river valley past the roofs of the neighbors' houses. The lack of outdoor space created by the dense surrounding residences is countered with design and creativity. Extended landings on the second floor provide hassle-free opportunities to enjoy the atmosphere of the outdoor and an adjoining strip of greenery, while the roof (accessed by an exterior staircase) makes for an ideal outdoor area to host family activities, or gatherings with friends.

The first floor, finished in concrete, flows outward to the landscape, not to exist beside it, but to become a part of it as a wraparound dry garden. Above, eaves extend in sections to provide shelter as one steps outdoor to enjoy nature. At the back of the house, a pocket of trees refreshes the senses and view; an old, stone kerb adds to the rustic charm of the scene and completes the woodland portrait. Glass doors connect the home to nature and invite the appealing view indoor to complement the candid, unconditional ambiance of the home.

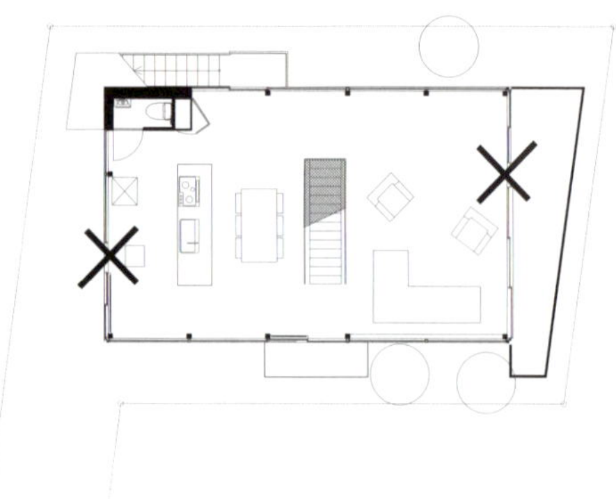

SECOND-FLOOR PLAN

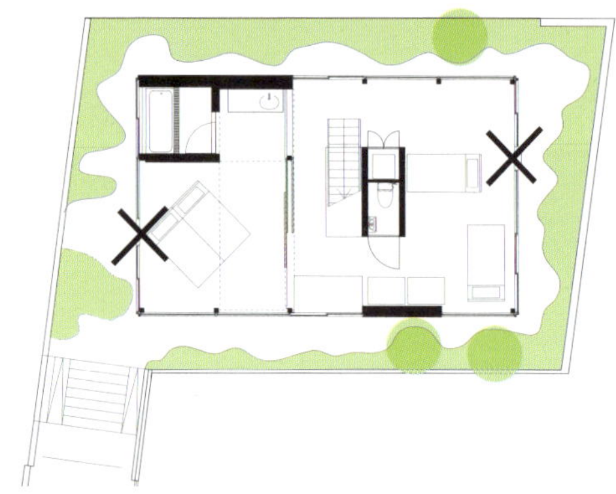

FIRST-FLOOR PLAN

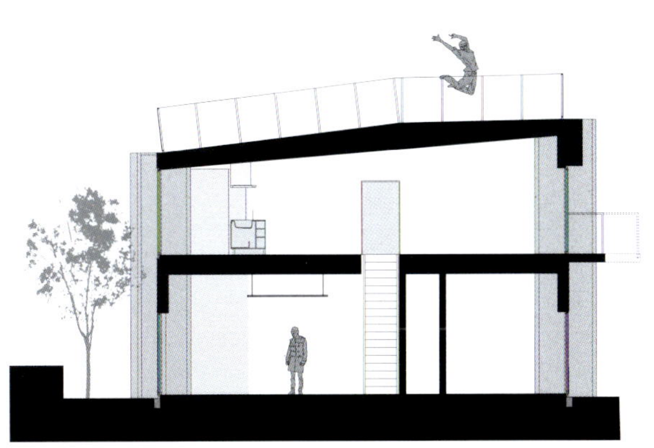

LONG SECTION

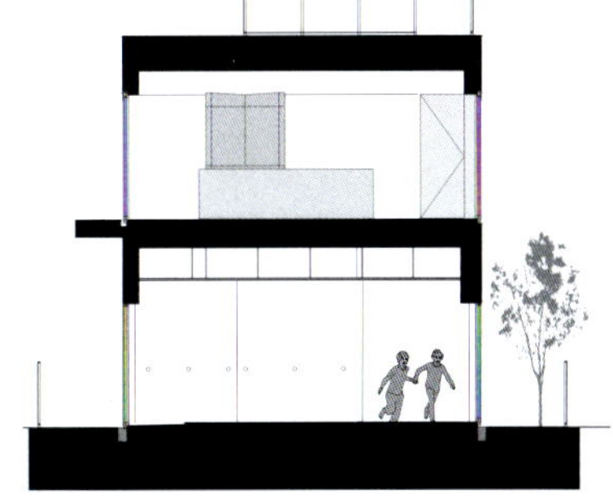

CROSS SECTION

Location /
Tokyo, Japan

Area /
968 square feet (89 square meters)

Completion /
2015

Design /
Ukei Shimada Architects Co., Ltd

Photography /
Ukei Shimada Architects Co., Ltd

House with Maple

Seasonal portraits of nature

Unperturbed by its compact site, this home provides a sense of spatial expanse with a creative plan and the helping hand of nature, for a lifestyle that is as enriched as it is pleasant. It confronts its densely populated surroundings in a built-up residential area in Tokyo with a placid and calm ambiance created through a flowing layout that imparts continuity within the home's traditional architecture.

At the request of the resident, a senior in her 90s, minimal functions team with a minimalist interior. The décor, though spartan, is inviting, featuring traditional elements—like a tatami room with *shoji* (Japanese screen door)—along rustic accents such as timber floors under exposed rafters and trusses. Essential living spaces are also planned with accessibility in mind—such as sliding doors—to facilitate ease of living within a limited range of activities.

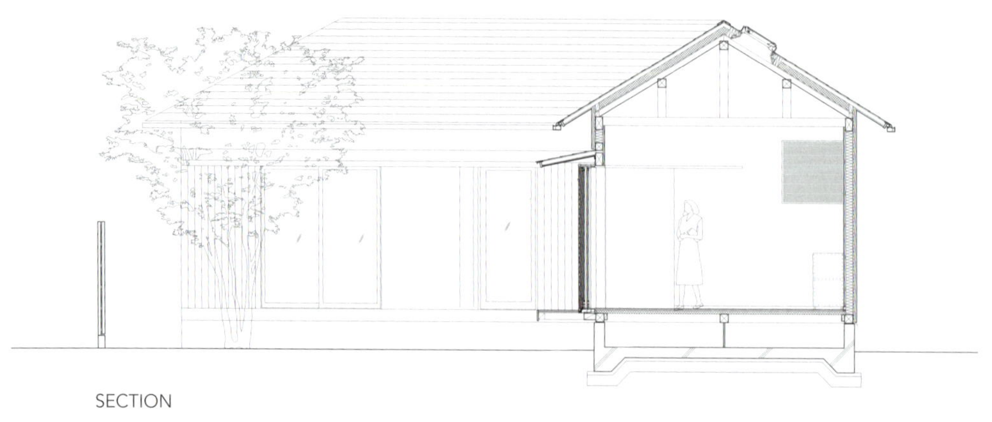

SECTION

The soul of the house is concentrated in three gardens. The building is planned in between these gardens and it arranges main spaces to extend the relation between activities within the home and the gardens. Framed against a shifting sky, active with the travel of clouds, the trees interact with the sun, the wind, and rain to create changing sceneries that share the joy of nature with the residents. Leading this green contingent is a maple tree that adorns the courtyard. A quiet beauty, it transforms with the seasons to fill the courtyard with colorful portraits throughout the year. In spring, vibrant, green leaves shimmy and sway in the breeze; in summer, a sun-kissed foliage gleams with a sheen; and in autumn, it is flushed in hues of auburn and amber, announcing the coming of winter. The maple's captivating metamorphosis sets the stage for a show of scenes that animates the home's ambiance.

Glass doors overlooking the courtyard and gardens connect the house to the nature outside and fill the home with abundant natural light. On the courtyard side, an *engawa* (veranda) under eaves enables the simple joy of the sun on the skin, or the fine mist of an airy drizzle on the face as one slows the pace and contemplates the transience of life, breathing in tandem with nature.

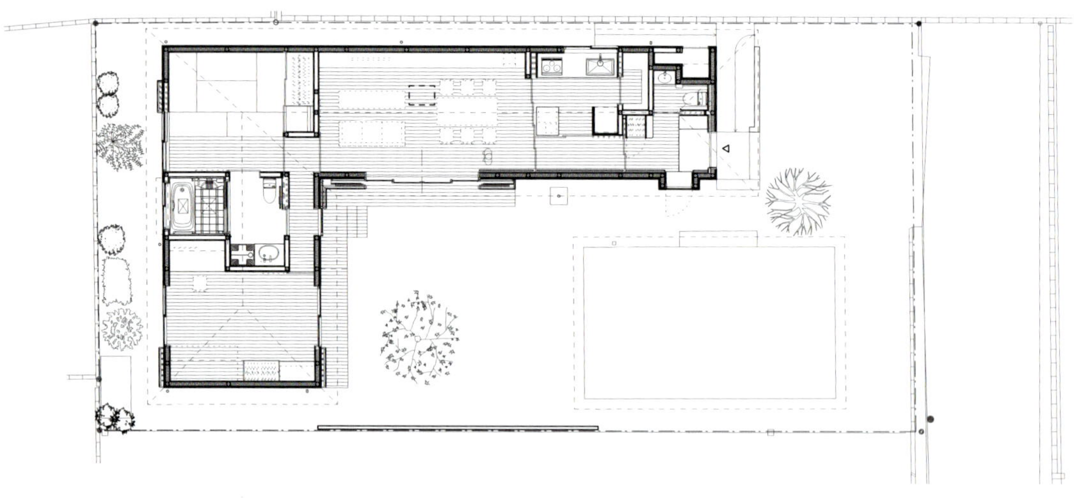

FLOOR PLAN

Location /
Saitama Prefecture, Japan

Area /
7,406 square feet (688 square meters)

Completion /
2018

Design /
Kohei Kudo & Associates

Photography /
Kai Nakamura

Higashimatsuyama House

Old, new, and nature

For over 300 years, generations of the homeowner's family have lived in this house (and in later years an added annex) that is snuggled by a pocket of primeval forest. Over the last years, the residents had managed well enough, shuttling back and forth between the main house and annex, however, a growing family and grandchildren announced the need for an upgrade.

The restoration retains the sentimental annex structure and cleverly marries old with new within blurred boundaries that integrate pockets of nature, articulating the entire ensemble as one, rather than a disjointed amalgam of buildings and scenery.

Two large roofs reorganize main living spaces to accommodate the various needs of the family. Placed at varying angles and height, they respond to the surroundings and the elements in an eye-catching, purposeful design: low eaves protect privacy and shield against glare, while high peaks scoop in natural light to create conducive areas for gathering and family activity around nature.

Enveloped by a natural forest, this home in the palm of nature weaves a nurturing ambiance that layers a kind of restorative calm with every leaf and every treetop. Gardens designed into the layout extend the breadth of the greenery and maintain a connection with the outdoor, even while indoors.

The garden at the front of the home is planted with an attractive mix of evergreen trees, bushes, and perennials to create depth in the landscape and adorn the home-front with a cozy, homely appearance. The deep tones of green dissipate into the lighter hues of a Zen-style lawn decorated with stepping-stones that trail from the outdoor terrace to the house. Arranged in a dispersed, staggered formation, the stepping-stones add a playfulness to the appreciation of the garden; as one stretches their stride to step on the stones, it encourages focus and gathers the attention, directing it away from external influences. It is also reminiscent of the free-spirited antics of childhood, welcoming a light-heartedness into the task. Another set of stepping-stones crosses a graveled

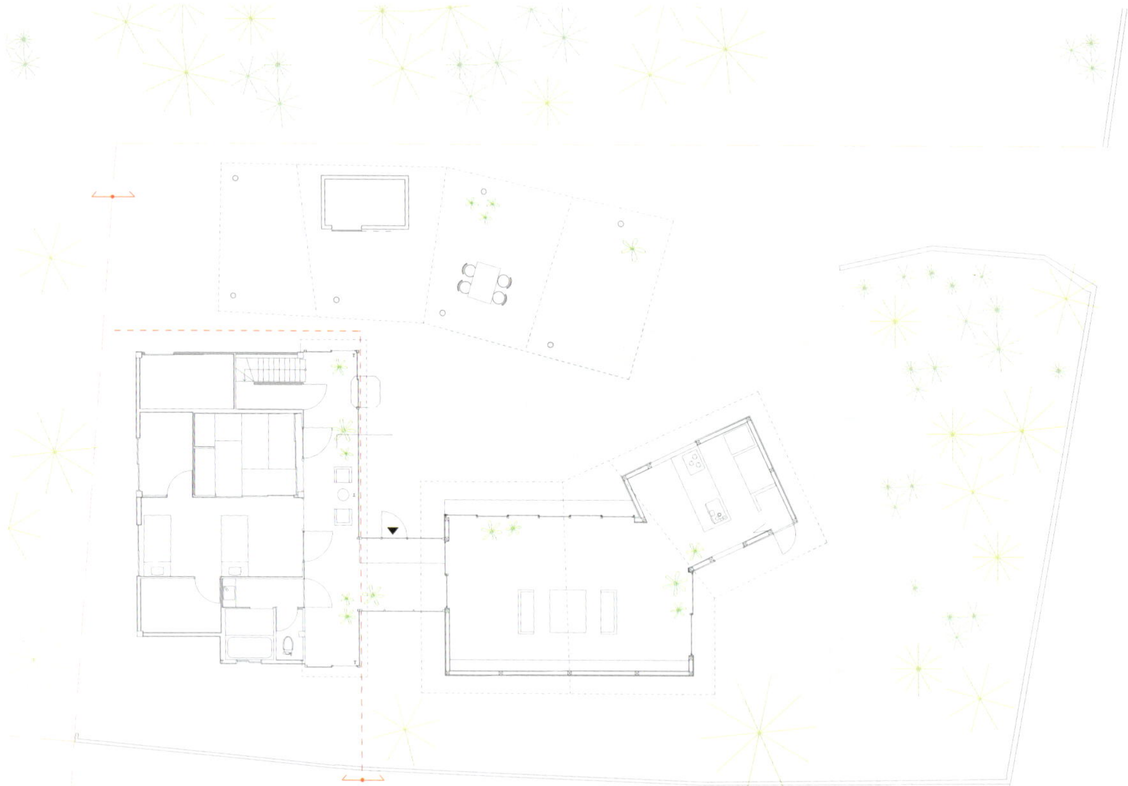

FLOOR PLAN

lane to the sun room, symbolizing a path that crosses through a stream, as was typically found in traditional Japanese strolling gardens. The graveled lane meanders around the home and site, expanding and narrowing in areas to symbolize the flow of water, as it would occur in a natural stream or river.

The sun room, a glassed, semi-outdoor area connects the main house to the annex and overlooks a side garden, integrating the outdoor with indoor, as it extends the home's living area to the outside. It also serves as an entrance hall that welcomes one home with a decompressing view of nature; certainly not a bad way to come home.

Location /
Nagano Prefecture, Japan

Area /
5,457 square feet (507 square meters)

Completion /
2019

Design /
CUBO design architect

Photography /
Koichi Torimura

T³

A play of shadows and scenery

Nestled atop a hill overlooking the Shonan coastline and the distant peaks of Mount Fuji, this home outlines quintessential Japanese architecture, blending the beautiful natural surroundings with its layout. Designed for a non-Japanese couple, this home realizes their long-time dream, bringing to the fore their love of Japanese gardens, while also incorporating their interest in Japanese culture and architecture. With a modern narration that intertwines with traditional Japanese building materials, such as granite, Japanese paper, black plaster, wood lattice, and warm timber, the home is also a novel experience for family and friends visiting from overseas, as it immerses them in the finer points of Japanese aesthetics within a serene and homely ambiance.

The façade is closed off from the street, emphasizing privacy, but on the other side, this hushed disposition is relinquished and the home becomes an escape from the mundane, or more fittingly, a surreal sanctuary. Glazed windows and sliding doors unveil a marvel of sceneries that flood the view as the home blissfully integrates with its majestic forest surroundings and glorious vistas. An alternating open-close layout cleverly blocks out the unwanted from sightlines and frames only spectacular views of relaxing nature.

Along the garden perimeter, continuous eaves—the defining element of Japanese Sukiya architecture—display their characteristic sharp, delicate accents in a contemporary steel outfit. A culmination of design and

functionality, they protect from the elements and extend over an *engawa* (varenda) that slips into a *karesansui* (dry garden) that circles the east corner of the house. Transfixing in its simple beauty, the garden stages a beautiful performance of shadows cast by the Tagyosho, a Japanese red pine tree, and the foliage of the forest backdrop, reflecting the pine's meticulous placement to exploit light. Veiled in scattered puddles of sunlight that mingle with drapes of shadows, the garden shows off a play of dark and light and mesmerizes the viewer together with the captivating borrowed scenery (*shakkei*)—a setting of lush greenery blended with the backdrop of Mount Fuji. Wide stepping-stones also trail pathways that lead exploration journeys, adding to the whimsical character of the garden. Connected to nature without inhibitions, this hybrid home is an embodiment of all things Japanese, speaking tradition and culture in a bold, modern voice of comfort.

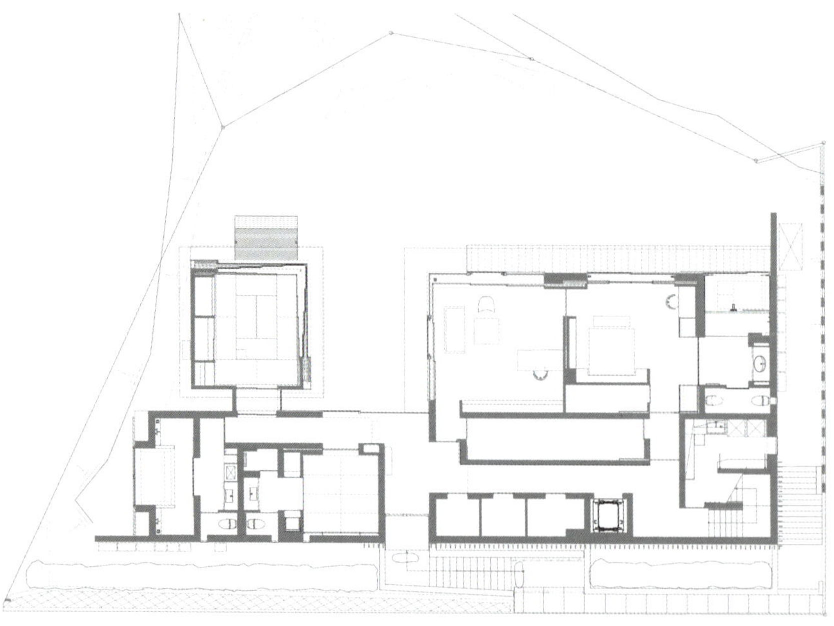

FIRST-FLOOR PLAN

Location /
Kobe, Japan

Area /
2,271 square feet (211 square meters)

Completion /
2014

Design /
Sqool Architect & Associates

Photography /
Yutaka Morimoto

House in Kobe

Courtyard with barbecue

This home in Kobe adds a barbecue to the garden with a renovation that also finishes the first floor as a large living space.

The redesign fits the home with a Japanese-style interior that highlights hardwood floors, lattices and tatami mats. No curtains interrupt this space, so as not to steal from its sense of expanse and integration with the outside and the garden.

An *engawa* (veranda) leads immediately to a courtyard to meet at one end, an intimate garden completed with gravel, stepping-stones, rock arrangements, and greenery, and on the other, a built-in, concrete barbecue pit that is set under an extended eave to protect it from rain that might ruin the cooking fire. The barbecue area, and by way of, the entire courtyard, can be accessed by both the dining area and living area through sliding doors, making for easy barbecue preparation and smooth guest-flow during gatherings. Stone benches provide seating around the barbecue pit and in a quiet corner of the garden so one can enjoy the peaceful environment with company, or privately, to set adrift deep thoughts. At the barbecue area, the bench is paired with a concrete tabletop that reaches out from the reverse side of the barbecue pit, making for a rustic outdoor dining nook.

At the garden side, ferns, shrubs, and small plants are dispersed between rock arrangements made up of rocks in different sizes and color to add depth and variety to the landscape. This scattering of greenery also creates a natural look for the garden, being similar to how plants grow in nature outdoors. A *tsukubai* (water basin) adds a historic accent to the scene that ties back to traditional garden arrangements, portraying old practices within contemporary creations. A Japanese maple completes the garden, taking its place in the center of the rock arrangements, announcing the intertwine of indoor and outdoor that is customary in traditional Japanese courtyards.

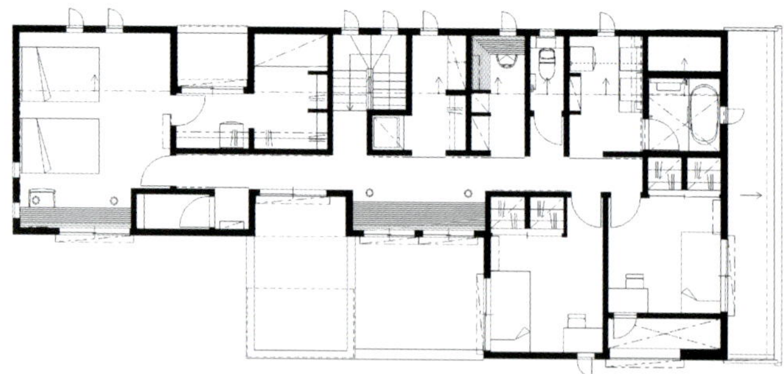

SECOND-FLOOR PLAN

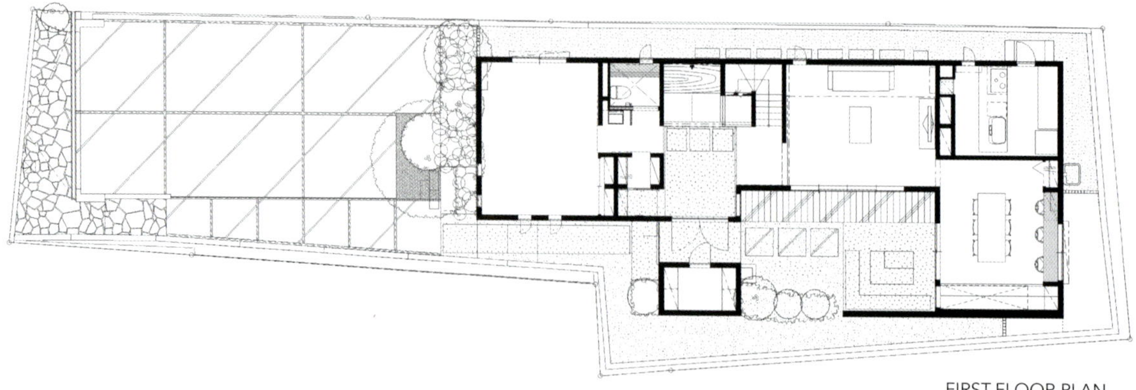

FIRST-FLOOR PLAN

Location /
Nagareyama, Chiba, Japan
Area /
2,017 square feet (187 square meters)
Completion /
2017

Design /
Yasumitsu Takano Architect & Associates
Photography /
Taku Hata

House in Minami-Nagareyama

Garden of stones

Set in the community-focused town of Nagareyama in Chiba Prefecture, this house is a haven of nature and quietude. Built a distance away from the road, it honors sightlines throughout that reach the garden outside and the blue skies beyond. Contrasting the urban cacophony of the modern day's technology-driven times, the home and its surroundings advocate a quieter, more natural way of life that takes joy in simple details, heritage, and cherishing nature's gifts.

Adding a breath of fresh, green air to the home, the home's park-like garden arranges trees and a mix of perennials and moss around aged stones that have since forgotten their natural beauty. Aptly translating the concept of *wabi sabi* (to take pleasure in simplicity and imperfection), the garden is constructed from recycled stones that were extracted from the old structure before renovation, as well as garden stones left behind by the homeowner's grandparents. In the stones' grooves, chips and cracks, and weathered patina, time is revealed and contemplated upon as one beholds their texture, formations, and color. The stones are used as they are, in their natural state, embracing their flaws—appreciating them, and even pronouncing them—through the play of light and shadows. Sometimes blending with the shivering shadows of trees that cloak them, and sometimes gleaming in shards of sunlight, the stones design an escape with nature, together with the vibrant green of the garden.

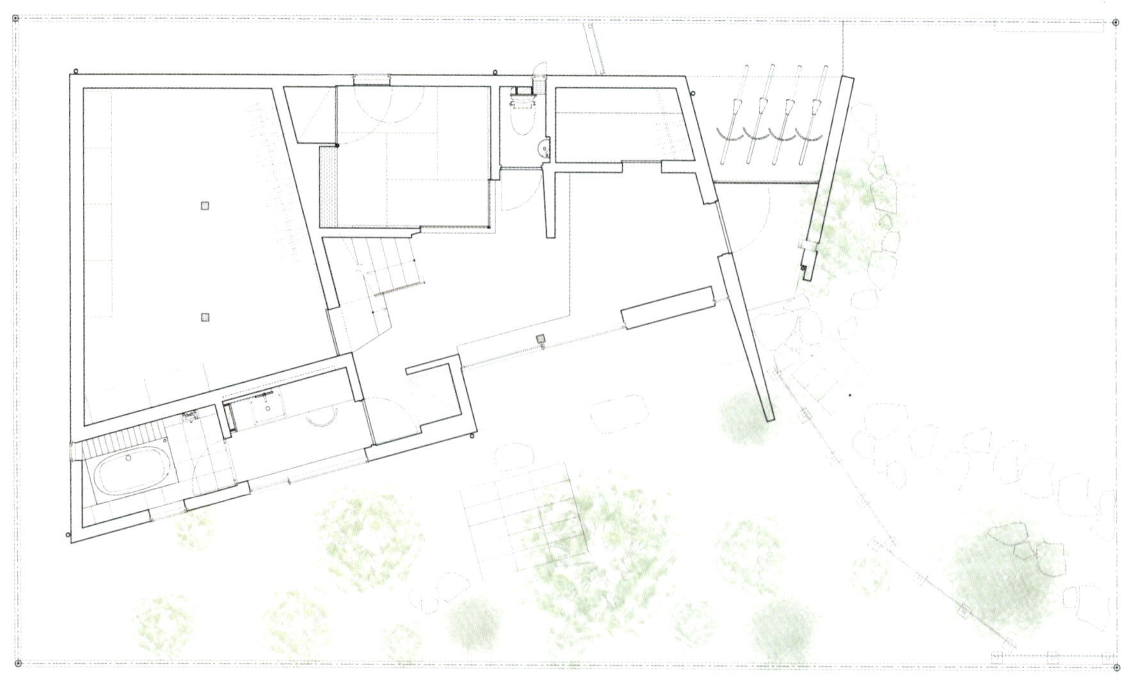

FIRST-FLOOR PLAN

Location /
Hiroshima Prefecture, Japan

Area /
818 square feet (76 square meters)

Completion /
2015

Design /
Fujiwaramuro Architects

Photography /
Toshiyuki Yano

House in Mukainada

A planted promenade

Accessible gardening is the focal point of the design in this home in Hiroshima for an elderly couple who loves greenery and tending their garden. Located in Mukainada residential district in Hiroshima, the single-story wooden home is set at an angle to its site perimeter to frame an uninterrupted view of the mimosa tree and mountain scenery at its street side, as well as enjoy natural daylight from the south. The home also considers a flexible plan that accommodates the potential for a store, gallery or workshop in the future.

Stepping-stones lead from the street to a circular, planted walkway that bands around the southwest exterior, completing its path through the home in the interior. Referencing a *doma*—a compacted-earth floor within traditional Japanese buildings—the walkway is a concrete structure at the home's exterior that finishes in pale wood in the interior. Contrasting the darker hue of the floor, the pale orbit in the interior enhances the home's aesthetic dimension, as it delineates interior spaces, setting apart a dining area at the center, a kitchen, bedroom, and bathroom further interior, and a recessed guestroom/office at the front.

Glass doors and windows connect the home to the outside and bring into the scene inside, the surrounding greenery. A mimosa tree outside the home is tasked to create privacy as it lends a refreshing view, while also blocking the view of the interior from the outside. The garden is expressed in polka-dots of greenery in the circular walkway and shrubs and small trees at the periphery. Planting beds in the walkway spring with lively plants and trees that are designed to grow with the home and its residents. Together with its companions of western red cedar, oak, and kempas, the garden will weather through time and evolve to transform the exterior attire of the house, possibly appearing different, but still with the same rejuvenating heart of green.

FLOOR PLAN

Location /
Nara, Japan

Area /
1,173 square feet (109 square meters)

Completion /
2011

Design /
Fujiwaramuro Architects

Photography /
Toshiyuki Yano

House in Sekiya

Around a courtyard to create all-around views

This single-story home is located in a residential district that offers little in view. The road that connects to the site is narrow and neighbors are situated in close proximity across the road; it also does not help that windows are lined up to face the road.

To create privacy, the design includes minimal outward-facing windows and doors, and instead, arranges the spaces around a central courtyard. Visible from all points in the house, the courtyard refreshes the visual scenery and floods the home with light, compensating for the lack of windows. To bring even more light into the home, the roof is detached from the structural walls, creating a perimeter of void space through which light filters in to illuminate spaces set further from the courtyard. Sliding glass doors around the courtyard channel the light flow into the inside of the home, while lending the peaceful courtyard scenery to the interior.

The courtyard garden is accompanied by an exterior garden—planted with Japanese ash, rhododendrons (azalea), and other perennials—which connects the home to the surrounding streetscape. A quaint bench set in the space provides a relaxing spot to decompress and tune out the world as one appreciates the greenery and the color parade of the evening sky.

In the interior, the design pays particular attention to sightlines from and toward each room, making sure that every space still enjoys privacy despite being visible through the courtyard: the children's room is set lower and the window in the tatami room is small and low. These design adjustments prevent lines of sight from confronting one another, to instead, create unique perspectives of the garden for each room.

SECTION

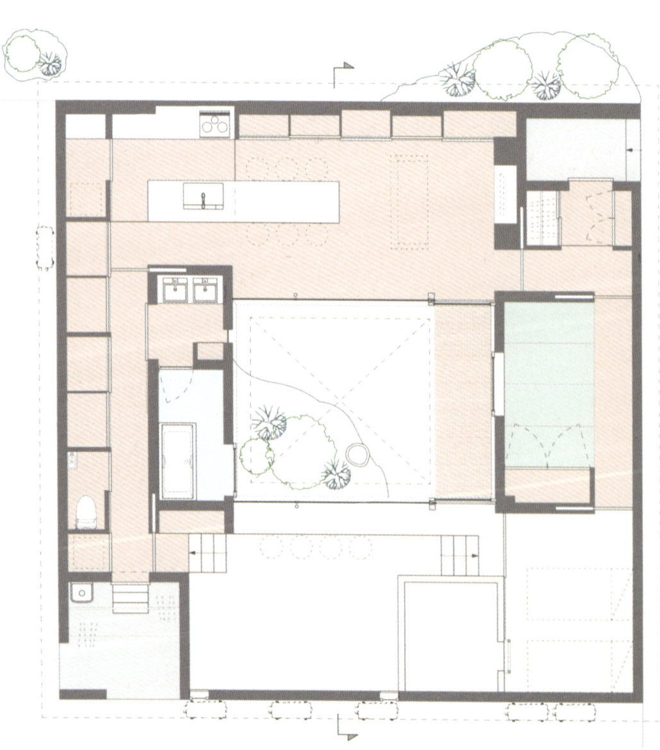

FLOOR PLAN

Location /
Kobe, Japan

Area /
1,496 square feet (139 square meters)

Completion /
2016

Design /
Tato Architects

Photography /
Shinkenchiku Sha

House in Tsukimiyama

Starting and ending with gardens

Interior and exterior intermingle in this house in Kobe, which sits in between two gardens. Corrugated metal cladding encloses spaces that spill into one another in an L-shaped plan that leads with a garden at the front of the house. Cocooned by neighboring buildings, the exterior appears like a courtyard that blends into the home, which flows past a courtyard at the back to an unusual annex-style bathroom and facilities nook at the rear. The courtyard links the main building to the annexed space, while also situating nature in the home to offer respite and rest.

Glass sash doors in light, wood fittings gently section the courtyard, while merging the area with the main living space through visual connections and a seamless flow. When opened, ventilation in the home is enhanced, as is the continuity and connection of the space. Designed as an area that can present as "inside" or "outside" through furniture arrangement, the courtyard fills the home with green energy and aspires to guide a design that effortlessly blends the indoor and outdoor, such that one can't differentiate where one ends and the other begins. Trees, ferns, and plants highlight the benefit of a planted courtyard in an urban home, which is usually closed-up and lacking light and ventilation; in this home, the courtyard garden is a nature retreat that provides welcome exposure to the outdoor, while still allowing privacy and shelter from the elements.

The bathroom annex is partitioned by green curtains that conceal a bathtub, while the facilities are candidly housed in a wooden wardrobe. A skylight brings light into the home and delights the greenery with sunshine. Doused in light, golden leaves glint amid spruces of green, staging pleasant portraits to accompany the day. Indoor, a main living area, kitchen and dining space span the first floor, with bedrooms located on the second. A wooden bridge connects the bedrooms to a workspace and toilet above the annex bathroom. Extending over the courtyard, the bridge allows alternative viewpoints of the calm greenery below as it unites the home along the concept of a blended space.

FIRST-FLOOR PLAN

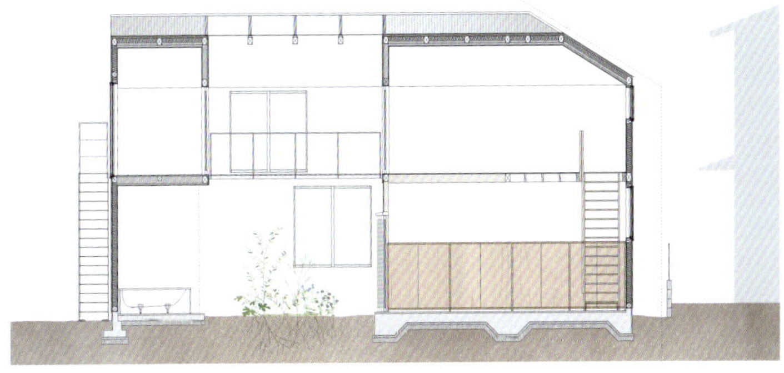

SECTION

Location /
Utsunomiya, Japan

Area /
1,523 square feet (141 square meters)

Completion /
2015

Design /
Yasumitsu Takano Architect & Associates

Photography /
Nobuyoshi Meguro, Yukinori Okamura

House in Utsunomiya

Green to the core

Facing a stretch of Keyaki (Japanese zelkova trees), this home keeps pace with its natural surroundings with a harmonious, woodland-inspired entrance garden that is composed with maple and oak trees, mossy rocks, ferns, and shrubs. The garden continues past the home's front and extends along the east side of the home's exterior to complement the existing nature near the site. Past the door, seeking eyes that have had a taste of the serene beauty at the entrance find more greenery to feast on. An open courtyard delivers a pleasant tree garden that is accented with traditional Japanese garden trims, such as a *tsukubai* (stone water basin), arranging a peaceful scenery that fills the home with a tranquil ambiance.

As eyes take in the quiet display, attention is diverted to the light streaming in from the window of the tatami room. Looking out at two different garden sceneries—the interior courtyard and the exterior garden connecting to the zelkova trees on site—the tatami room is a sanctuary that realigns the mind and reconnects the soul. The low windows and plaster-finish ceiling serve to enhance the intimacy and quietude of the space, creating a grounding point as the plan meanders through varying sceneries of indoor and outdoor.

The living room enjoys a view of the zelkova trees set against blue sky and the dining area samples natural light channeled in through a skylight above. Rooms on the second floor feature window seating, so one can appreciate the relaxing gardens and surroundings. A paved terrace overlooking the courtyard completes the home with a sheltered outdoor space where one can enjoy the elements for a relaxing reprieve from the hustle of urban life. As the breeze whispers by and light shifts across the courtyard garden to frame different depths of sceneries, heart and home join as one.

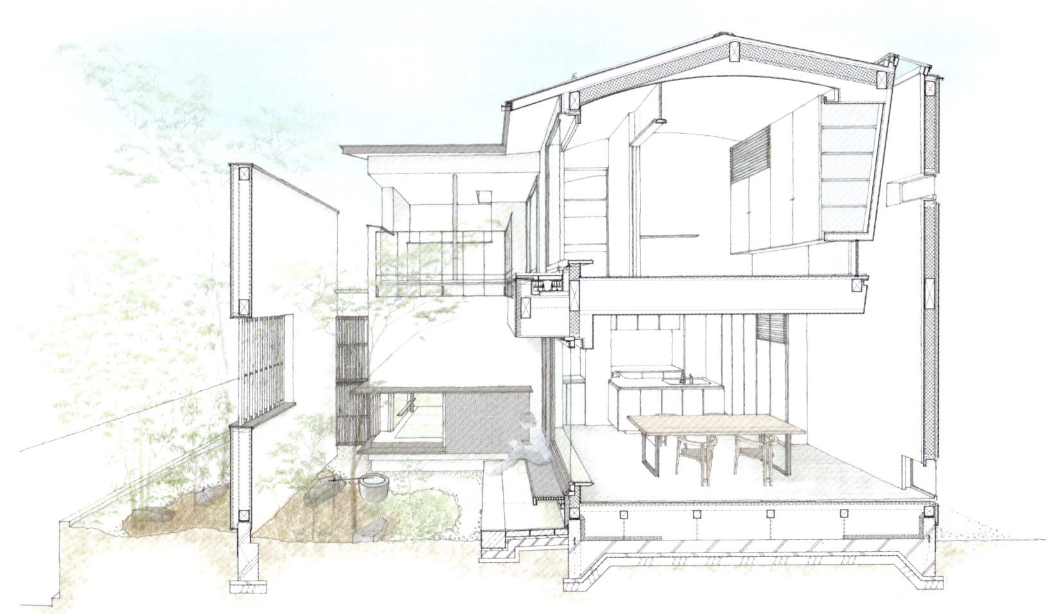

SECTION

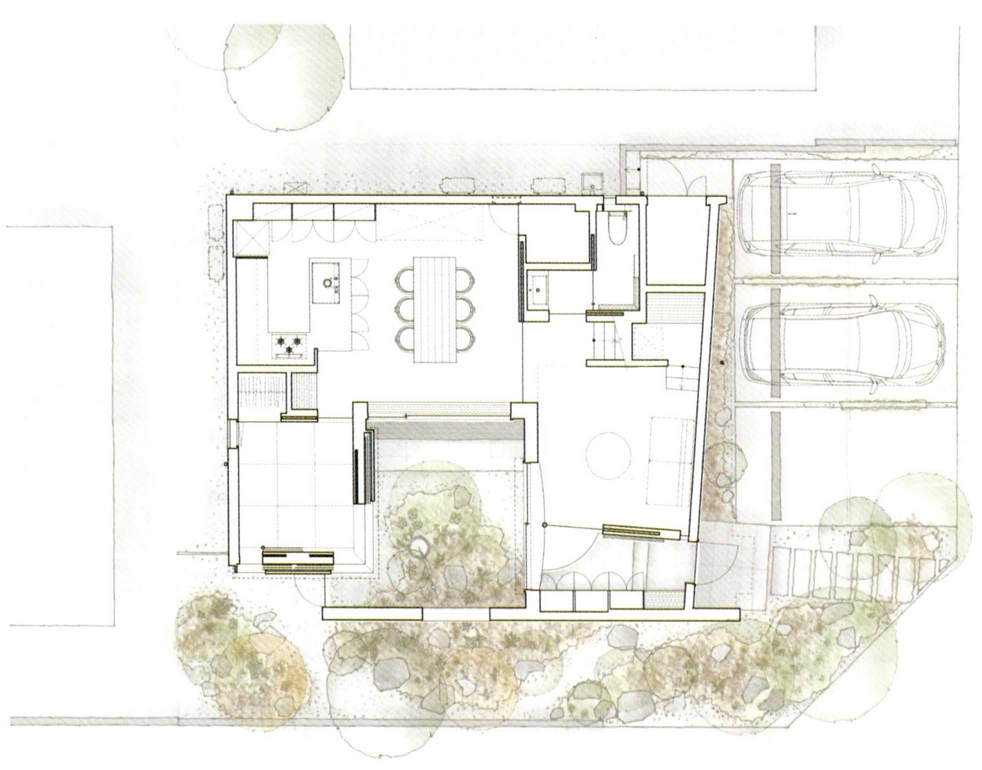

FIRST-FLOOR PLAN

SECOND-FLOOR PLAN

Location /
Nagareyama, Japan

Area /
947 square feet (88 square meters)

Completion /
2017

Design /
ikmo

Photography /
Masao Nishikawa

Nagare House

Mixing past into present

Contradicting typical Japanese home architecture that usually features fortified outer shells to enhance earthquake safety, this house in a suburban hillside neighborhood in Nagareyama, Chiba, incorporates traditional Japanese building and design techniques that observe modern interpretations. This design approach naturally links the house with the topography and surrounding buildings, as well as the time spans and history of the neighborhood.

Though most houses in this 40-year-old neighborhood have been rebuilt, many still dot the sloping streets with eye-catching hipped roofs and inviting gardens. This home matches its surrounding vibe and land contours, and at the same time establishes new relationships with the environment and community by sampling building traditions of the past. The interior and exterior are linked in agreement through a *doma*, which translates literally to "dirt place," usually referring to an area of compacted land in traditional Japanese homes or buildings that extends the entryway—in short, the space between indoor and outdoor.

The open-air *doma* creates a semi-exterior area that flows both outward and inward. Extending outward, it blends the home with the garden outside, breaking down concrete into stepping-stones that disintegrate into the clover-covered hills of the front garden that interpret the Japanese courtyard. Trees in the garden and around the site add their magic touch to create a lush scenery that highlights the open, relaxed ambiance of the home, recalling architectures of old Japan, which seamlessly and joyfully blended into their rural landscapes of rice paddies and farm fields.

Progressing inward, the *doma* disappears under a spacious roof to meet a large table that combines the kitchen and dining area, while also serving as a worktop for cooking preparation, a desk for work, a dining table, and stairs to the second floor. Activities in the home revolve around this table and expand into other spaces, such as the raised sitting area that combines wood and tatami flooring. A window wraps around a corner of the living area and looks out to the garden to remind of the greenery outside and continue the relaxing scenery indoor. As it weaves seldom-observed architectural traditions like the *doma*, a large roof and an *irori* (sunken hearth) into modern day, this quaint home honors the past and continues it into the future.

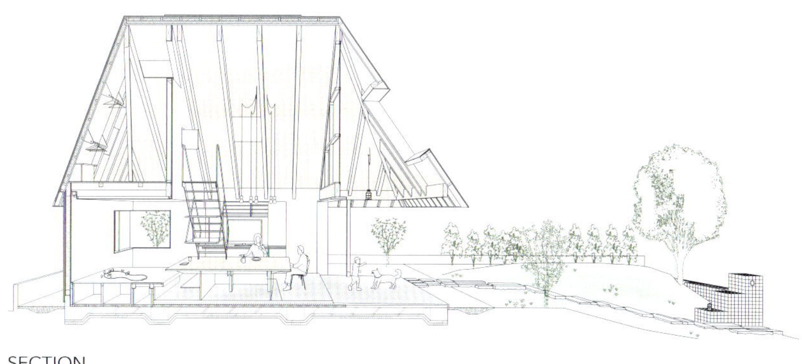

SECTION

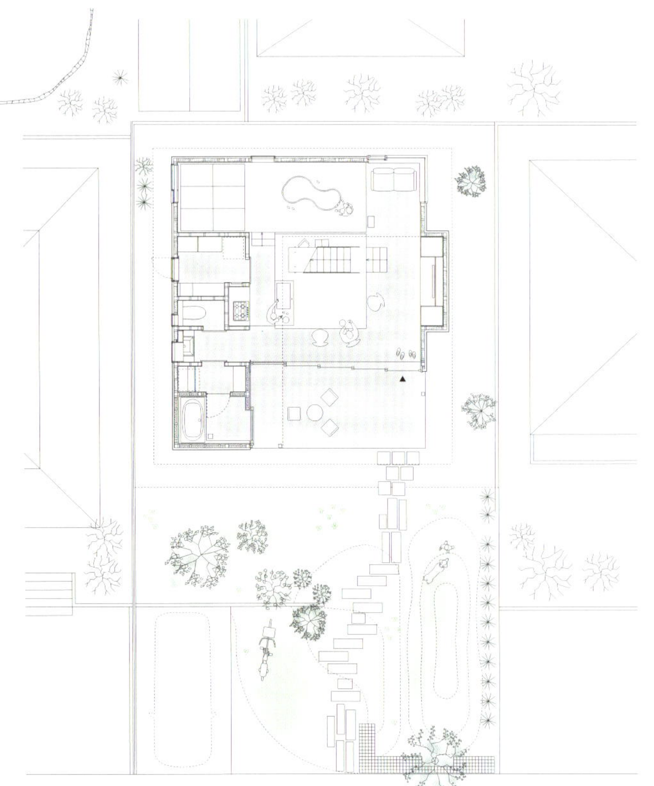

FIRST-FLOOR PLAN

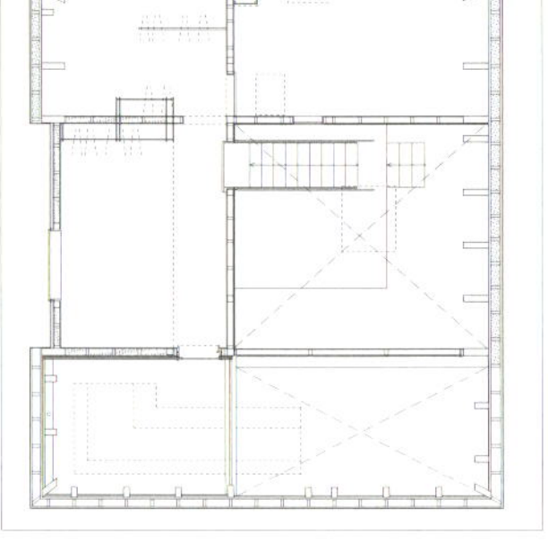

SECOND-FLOOR PLAN

Location /
Yokohama, Kanagawa, Japan

Area /
2,282 square feet (212 square meters)

Completion /
2018

Design /
acaa

Photography /
Ueda Hiroshi

Recollecting the Topography

Hillocks, lanes, and green spaces that unite

This two-family house built in the suburbs is surrounded by apartments to the north and east, creating the feeling of being in everyone's view. Gardens designed into the plan and distributed within the site counter the dense surroundings and provide privacy, so that freedom within the home and lifestyles of choice need not be compromised. Beyond that, the gardens also provide ideal venues for both families, who belong to two different generations, to come together, so that they may build stronger relations and bonds between them.

The home is divided into two volumes, each accommodating a different family; the gardens bring the two generations together, bridging the gap to connect them in an inviting space that is immersed in peaceful, lush greenery. A hill constructed from soil dug up during the construction of the foundation, together with pockets of greenery that sometimes sneak into connecting lanes on the site to design rustic, rural pathways, shape a three-dimensional landscape. This landscape gives depth to the house when viewed from the road; the trees planted here also contribute to the inviting front of the neighborhood.

The volumes' isolated organization, independant of each other, allows the windows of each volume to be placed without facing each other, thereby maintaining a level of separateness to enable a less conscious existence. Privacy is extended further through the volumes' non-uniform first-floor height. Set 3 feet (1 meter) apart—with the first floor of one volume built lower than first floor of the other volume—this height difference creates different eye-levels that shield each volume (and its inhabitants) from the other's direct line of sight. The result is an environment in which the two generations either look up or down to see each other, creating a sense of distance and seclusion within their own unique quarters.

SECTION

FIRST-FLOOR PLAN

Location /
Fukuoka, Japan

Area /
1,776 square feet (165 square meters)

Completion /
2018

Design /
acaa

Photography /
Ueda Hiroshi

Visual Metaphors of Design

A resort vacation at home

Surrounded on three sides with residential developments, privacy is a key concern in this home with neighboring residences peering down at it. A variety of lifestyle spaces are cleverly placed behind shielding gardens strewn across the home, which also double as enhancers that raise the aesthetics of the home, transforming the space into a tasteful, suburban retreat.

Not only do they add color and life to the home, the courtyards also act as lightwells that pull natural light into the interior, while enhancing ventilation. The front terrace welcomes with an attractive tapestry of shadows stitched together by lush bamboo trees and a slated screen that recalls the design of the fence at the entrance. A skylight takes the welcome up a notch by drenching the living room in an abundance of light to put forth a cheery greeting; sceneries of the gardens around the home join in to provide an instant sense of relaxation. The interior space evokes the atmosphere of a resort, with white painted walls, dark cabinetry and wood beams, and openings in the space that connect to the outdoor to deliver portraits of nature's handiwork. A high ceiling on the second floor lifts the ambiance of the space further as it imbues the home with a feeling of expanse.

Complementing the openness of the space with a more intimate embrace is the tatami room, which extends a cozier experience. Utilizing the varying heights of the site, it is set lower than the main living space. As one descends stairs to enter this room, a sense of privacy and seclusion is felt. The mood is elevated again approaching the rooftop, which provides an ideal location for family activities. Standing under the open sky and looking upon the gardens, it's easy to forget the busy surroundings and be one with the moment, connecting with nature and its wonders.

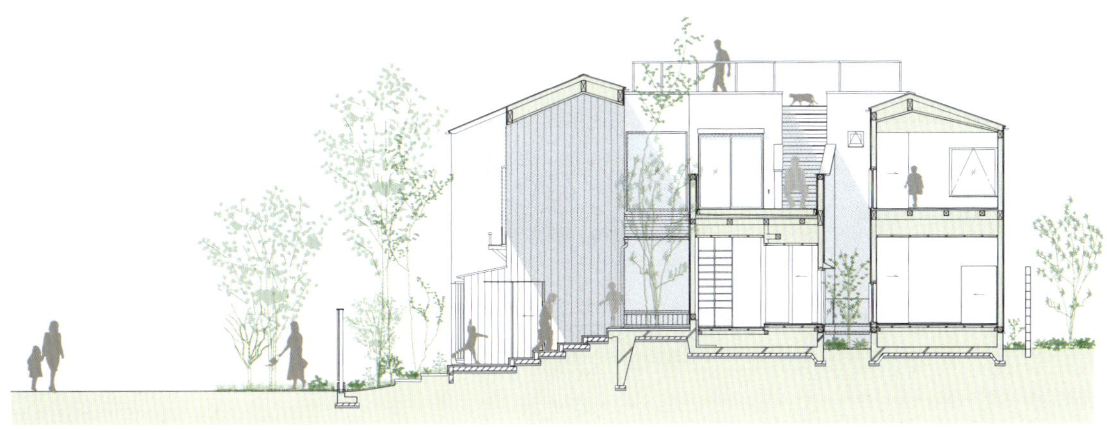

LONG SECTION

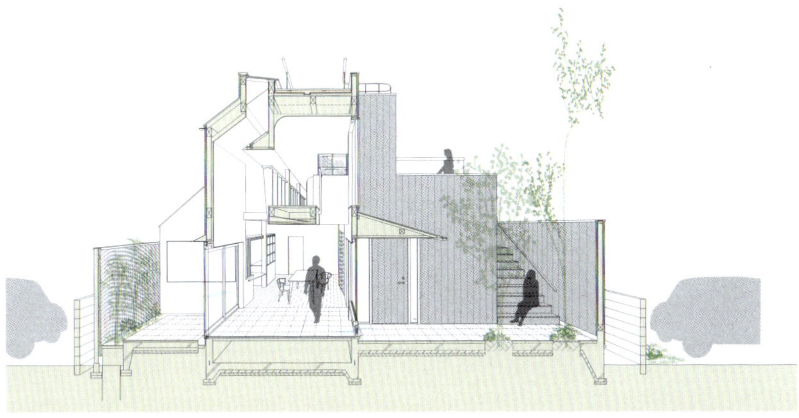

CROSS SECTION

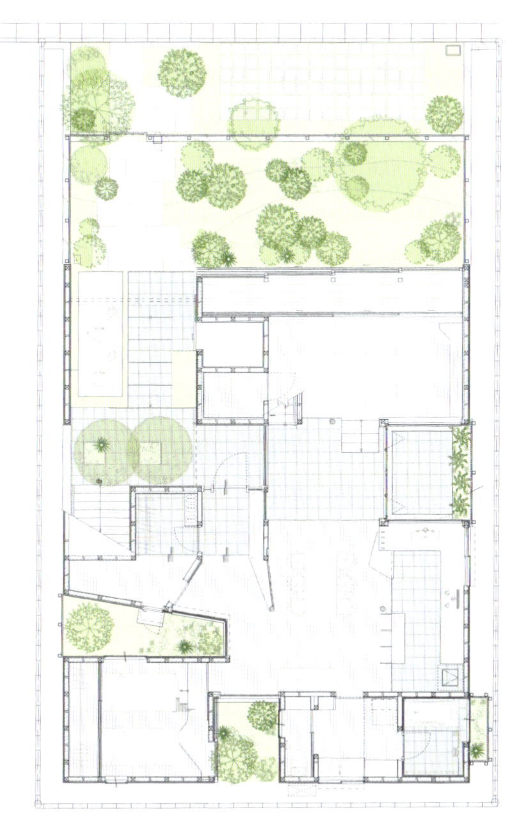

FIRST-FLOOR PLAN

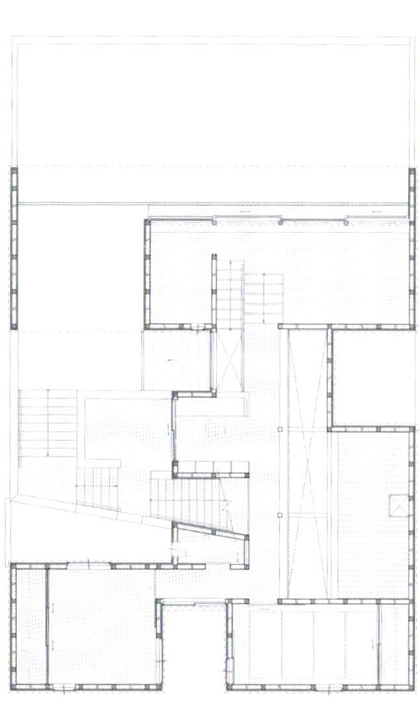

SECOND-FLOOR PLAN

Location /
Matsudo, Chiba, Japan

Area /
1,550 square feet (144 square meters)

Completion /
2019

Design /
DOG

Photography /
Nao Takahashi

Acquired Stilt House

Courtyards among pilotis

This modern stilt house contradicts the origin of the architectural concept somewhat, sitting on an artificially constructed site, very unlike the usual character of stilt houses, which are mostly built on earth-derived sites such as a wetland or a slope. Being so, it factors in two retaining walls in the south and east, and a block ridge on the south. The texture of these walls is incorporated into the design of the piloti space, which spans the extent of the home. Apart from creating striking aesthetics, the stilt design also protects the home against moisture damage and unwanted visits from bug life, which is useful in the spring and summer seasons when critters are out and about exploring.

The first-floor piloti space accommodates courtyards that weave in between the pilotis, adding warmth to the home with greenery. The main living spaces on the second floor look out onto these courtyards through sliding glass windows and draw these lively sceneries of nature into the home to accompany the residents as they move within the space.

The house adapts its single volume to the artificially constructed site with yard spaces and concrete ledges that seem to spill from the formwork. These ledges perform as seats that allow full use of the first-floor piloti space, providing opportunities to sit, relax, appreciate the gardens and commune with nature. Built around these courtyards, the living space on the second floor is treated to ample natural light and ventilation. As tall trees in the courtyards reach for the sun, leafy branches peek through windows into the living area on the second floor and share the calming beauty of nature with everyday life.

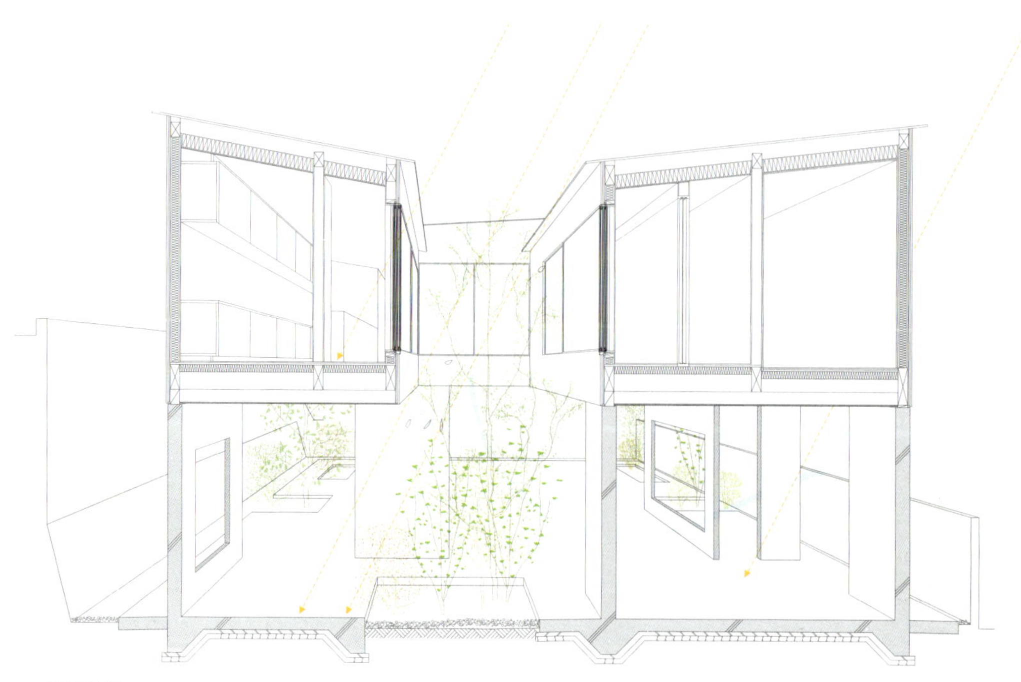

SECTION

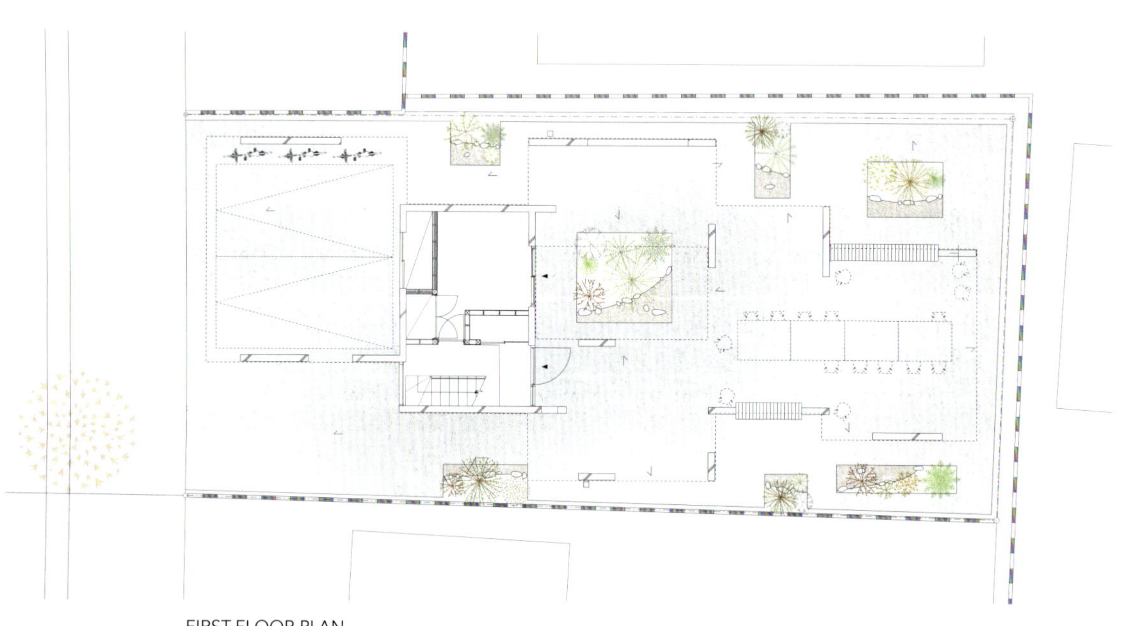

FIRST-FLOOR PLAN

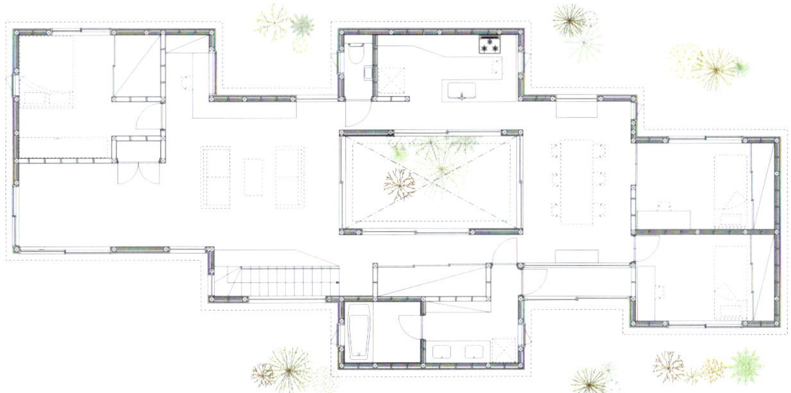

SECOND-FLOOR PLAN

Index

Published in Australia in 2021 by
The Images Publishing Group Pty Ltd
ABN 89 059 734 431

Offices

Melbourne
6 Bastow Place
Mulgrave, Victoria 3170
Australia
Tel: +61 3 9561 5544

New York
6 West 18th Street 4B
New York, NY 10011
United States
Tel: +1 212 645 1111

Shanghai
6F, Building C, 838 Guangji Road
Hongkou District, Shanghai 200434
China
Tel: +86 021 31260822

books@imagespublishing.com
www.imagespublishing.com

The Images Publishing Group Reference Number: 1591

A catalogue record for this book is available from the National Library of Australia

Title: The Intimate Beauty of a Japanese Courtyard
Author: Hitoshi Saruta (Introduction)
ISBN: 9781864708981

Printed by Everbest Printing Investment Limited, in Hong Kong/China